KU-097-586

trotman

GETTING INTO

Art & Design

COURSES

3rd Edition

LEARNING RESOURCES CENTRE

Havering College
of Further and Higher education

Jonathan Hollins & James Burnett

378.42   AG   164793

Index of advertisers

Getting into Art and Design Courses
This third edition published in 2006 by Trotman and Company Ltd
2 The Green, Richmond, Surrey TW9 1PL

© Trotman and Company Limited 2006

Editorial and Publishing Team
Author Jonathan Hollins and James Burnett
Editorial Mina Patria, Editorial Director; Rachel Lockhart, Commissioning Editor; Catherine Travers, Managing Editor; Ian Turner, Editorial Assistant
Production Ken Ruskin, Head of Manufacturing and Logistics; James Rudge, Production Artworker
Sales and Marketing Suzanne Johnson, Marketing Manager
Advertising Tom Lee, Commercial Director; Sarah Talbot, Advertising Sales Manager

British Library Cataloguing in Publication Data
A catalogue record for this book is available from the British Library

ISBN 1 84455 077 X

All rights reserved. No part of this publication may be reproduced, stored in a retrieval system or transmitted in any form or by any means, electronic and mechanical, photocopying, recording or otherwise without prior permission of Trotman and Company Ltd.

Typeset by Mac Style, Nafferton, E. Yorkshire
Printed and bound in Great Britain by Bell & Bain Ltd, Glasgow, Scotland

Founded in 1973, **Mander Portman Woodward (MPW)** is one of the UK's best-known groups of independent sixth-form colleges with centres in London, Birmingham and Cambridge. It offers over 40 subjects at AS and A2 with no restrictions on subject combinations and a maximum class size of eight.

MPW has one of the highest numbers of university placements each year of any independent school in the country. It has developed considerable expertise over the years in the field of applications strategy and has produced **MPW Guides** covering entrance procedures in Medicine, Dentistry, Veterinary Science, Physiotherapy, Psychology, Business & Management, Law and Art & Design courses. On a more general level there is a guide to help applicants complete their UCAS applications, a guide on Oxford and Cambridge, a guide on American Universities, and a guide to examination success. We are grateful to Trotman and Company for helping us to make the Guides available to a wider audience.

If you would like to know more about MPW or MPW Guides, please telephone us on 020 7835 1355 or visit www.mpw.co.uk

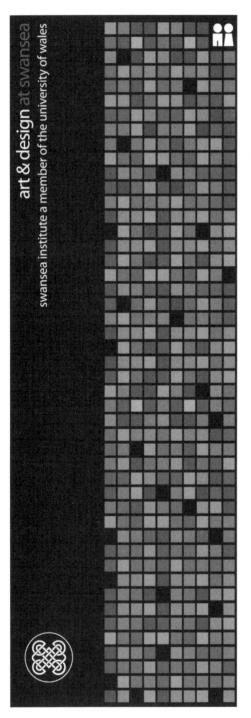

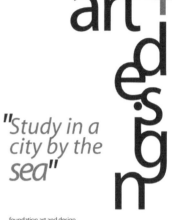

"Study in a city by the sea"

foundation art and design

BA(Hons) art history and visual arts practice*
BA(Hons) design for advertising
BA(Hons) fine art - ceramics
BA(Hons) fine art- combined media
BA(Hons) fine art- painting and drawing
BA(Hons) general illustration
BA(Hons) graphic design
BA(Hons) joint honours: art history
BA(Hons) photography in the arts
BA(Hons) photojournalism
BA(Hons) surface pattern design
BA(Hons) surface pattern design-textiles for fashion
BA(Hons) surface pattern design-textiles for interiors
BA(Hons) video
BA(Hons) documentary video*
BA(Hons) video arts*

taught masters portfolio
MA fine art
MA photography
MA visual arts enterprise
MA visual comunication

research degrees ; MPhil, PhD

for details please contact
01792 481285

www.sihe.ac.uk
artanddesign@sihe.ac.uk
* subject to validation

CONTENTS

ACKNOWLEDGEMENTS

This book would not have been possible without the involvement of a great many people. In particular, I would like to thank Jonathan Hollins, who was the main contributor to, and driving force behind, the first edition of this book, and Beryl Dixon for her work on the second edition and earlier publications. Thank you also to Colin Kerrigan and Robert Green from the University of the Arts London, Rosemary Allen at the University of Hertfordshire, Bill Watson at Camberwell College of Arts, and David Girling and Sarah Horton at Norwich School of Art and Design for their help and expertise, advice and written contributions. The tutors who are part of MPW's art-school preparation programme provided invaluable advice and expertise: they are Mark Cheeseman, Louise De La Hey, Kate Brett, Lisa Marklew, Kevin Newark, Alan Shaw and Gerard Hastings. And finally, thank you to Jenny Park and Thuy Nguyen, to the other students who contributed to the book, and to Rachel Lockhart at Trotman for her advice.

Postgraduate Opportunities

winchester
school of
art

University
of Southampton

For further information
Call 023 8059 4741, email
prospenq@sotonac.uk or visit
www.wsa.soton.ac.uk

MA Fine Art
• Fine Art by Project
• Painting
• Printmaking
• Sculpture

MA Design
• Advertising Design Management
• Communication Design
• Fashion and Textiles by Project
• Fashion Management
• Textile Design
• Textile and Fibre Art

MRes Digital Arts and Design
• Digital Architecture and
  Landscape Modelling
• Digital Game Design

MA Museums & Galleries:
• Access & Learning*
• Archives in Museums*
• Culture, Collections &
  Communication
• Collections Management
• History of Textiles & Dress
• Interpreting Historic Interiors*

MA Textile Conservation

MA Organics Conservation

MRes Science and Heritage*

trotman

Expert advice on how
to complete your
application correctly and
to your best advantage.

For more details and
to order:
call 0870 900 2665
or visit
www.trotman.co.uk

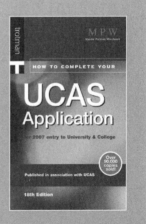

trotman

M P W
Mander Portman Woodward

HOW TO COMPLETE YOUR

UCAS
Application

for 2007 entry to University & College

Over
90,000
copies
sold!

Published in association with UCAS

18th Edition

new edition £9.99

M P W
Mander Portman Woodward

Introduction

When Simon Starling won this year's Turner Prize for his work that included a piece called Shedboatshed (he dismantled a shed and made it into a boat which, after paddling it down a river, he turned back into a shed), many people asked the question: is this art? The Turner Prize has stimulated arguments about the nature of art for a number of years, as have works such as Damien Hirst's *Away from the Flock* (a stuffed sheep preserved in formaldehyde) and Tracey Emin's *My Bed*. Whatever the merits of Emin's piece, without the skills and abilities of practitioners from a wide variety of disciplines within the field of art and design, it would not have existed and you would not be reading about it now. Throughout its life, from conception to production, exhibition and review, *My Bed* has been touched by artists and designers. A Fine Artist, Emin came up with the idea and oversaw its realisation, furniture designers designed the bed, textile designers were responsible for the linen, an architect designed the building in which the piece was exhibited, a communications specialist designed the catalogue, and art historians and critics reflected on its successes and failures, to name but a few of those involved.

In applying to art school you are taking the first step towards what will hopefully become not only your chosen career but also a lifetime journey of experimentation, invention and discovery. Perhaps you already have a strong feeling for a particular discipline, such as fine art, film or fashion and textiles. Or maybe you are unsure which discipline is for you but just know that your instinct to work with colour, line, form, shape and pattern, to question, experiment and explore is something that you have to develop. Either way, this book is specifically designed for you.

WHAT IS THIS BOOK ABOUT?

Which course(s) should I take? Where should I apply to study? What should I include in my portfolio? How do I prepare for an interview? This book offers practical answers to these questions and many others, and aims to guide you successfully through the application process.

WHO IS THIS BOOK FOR?

This book covers the procedure for applications for both Foundation Studies and undergraduate degree courses in Art and Design. If you are a student currently studying at A level you will find all chapters of this guide relevant. However, if you are studying for a Vocational A level (AVCE), BTEC National Diploma or similar qualification you may be tempted not to read the chapter on Foundation courses (page 5). I strongly suggest that you do read it – partly because it will help you to know what other students have been up to and also because it contains a section on how to choose a college. Although guidance on how to choose a course is provided in the chapter 'Degree courses', you will find this information helpful.

If you are a student applying from outside the UK or a mature student you will have additional special considerations. Most of what is contained in this book will apply, and there is additional information in Chapter 6 and the 'Non-standard applicants' section in Chapter 5.

Throughout the book I have illustrated the entrance procedures by referring to A levels. The information is equally relevant to students studying Scottish Highers, the

International Baccalaureate or the Irish Leaving Certificate. If you have any questions about whether your academic qualifications will satisfy the art schools, you should contact them directly.

HOW TO USE
THIS BOOK

Read it. No, really! Just having the book on the shelf won't get you into college. Discuss the ideas and information contained within it. Speak to your tutors, friends and parents. You will find it helpful to talk things through. Certain chapters have checklists with tick boxes: use these to help you keep track of your progress. Space is also provided for making notes. Above all, take action – and when you have finished the book you should have a clear idea of where action is needed. If, for example, you realise that you probably need to do some more life drawing, then go and do some. Admissions tutors are, in any case, always interested in work applicants have done in their own time – i.e. not just pieces they have done for A level coursework or exam. Make every effort to visit potential colleges. It would be like taking a lucky dip and hoping for the best, to

ROUTES FOR ART STUDENTS

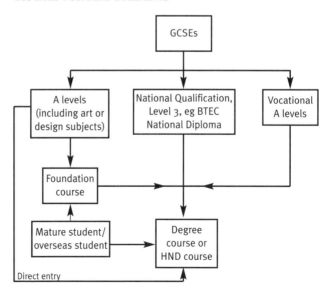

pick courses and colleges unseen and then to find out to your horror when you are called for interview that you would be unable to bear the place for one, three or four years! You will feel far more confident about your application if you know that you have done everything that you possibly can to help yourself.

1

Foundation courses

Art and Design Foundation courses – the full name is Level 3 Diploma in Foundation Studies (Art and Design) – provide a bridge between the kind of study undertaken at GCSE and A level and the type of work you will do on courses offered at degree level. Although there are exceptions, for those of you currently studying general A levels and hoping to get into art school, taking up a place on a Foundation course will be your next step. Most typically, they are self-contained one-year courses available at a variety of different types of institution, including universities, art schools and colleges of further and higher education.

Why do I need to do a Foundation course?

For those of you who have not completed a Vocational A level or BTEC National Diploma in Art and Design, studying on a Foundation course will give you an opportunity to find out much more about your creative interests and abilities. You will have the chance to experiment with methods and materials which will not have been previously available. You will have the freedom to explore your own ideas and will be truly working for yourself. You can expect to have a lot of fun. While each course will have its own individual style and content may vary, all Foundation courses will attempt to challenge and develop your critical awareness and creative skills. They will help you to select a specialist area of study, prepare your portfolio and make applications for degree courses. There is probably no better way to prepare for a specialist degree course than by completing Foundation studies. Take a look at the views of a student.

Alice Williams, final-year A level student 'Applying for a place on an Art and Design Foundation course felt like the next step on the ladder for me. I was still unsure of which career path to go down but knew that I loved art and wanted to pursue it in the future. The great thing about the Foundation course is that you can use it in whatever art-based career you choose: it's an extra year in which to explore your artistic talents, have fun and move closer to fulfilling your ambitions. Although I had experimented with a variety of media during my A level, I didn't feel that I had done so to my full potential. A Foundation course gives you the opportunity to experiment further and, most importantly, helps you to discover your true abilities.'

WHAT CAN YOU EXPECT FROM A FOUNDATION COURSE? Colleges vary in the ways in which they organise their courses, but in nearly all cases you will choose from the following areas of study:

- Art – painting, sculpture and drawing – could also include film and photography.
- Communication – graphic design, illustration and time-based media.
- Design – ceramics, metals, fashion and product design.

Course content is standardised to a certain extent, in accordance with the regulations of one of three awarding bodies that validate courses in England, Wales and Northern Ireland. These are ABC Awards, Edexcel and the Welsh Joint Education Committee (WJEC). Under their regulations, Foundation courses are divided into three phases, each phase being roughly equivalent to one of the three terms that make up the academic year.

The *exploratory phase* will give you a general introduction to the theory and practice of art and design. You will have the chance to experiment with a wide range of materials you may not have had the opportunity to use before – including plaster, wood, metal and ceramics, for example, and will work on projects designed to help you to identify your strengths and interests.

In the second or *pathway phase* you will investigate a specialist area of art and design practice, guided by a tutor experienced in that field. At this stage of the course you will also begin to put together a portfolio for degree-course applications.

Last comes the *confirmatory phase* during which you will complete your portfolio, work on a major project normally negotiated with your specialist tutor and put together a final show. The Foundation course exhibition might include static exhibits, multimedia displays and a fashion show.

During the confirmatory stage you will be expected to produce a *personal confirmatory study*. The following is an extract from ABC guidelines, stating what this should consist of:

'Candidates must include in their portfolio of artwork evidence that they can:

- Research and negotiate a project brief which enables their skills to be clearly demonstrated.
- Plan and manage their own project effectively to produce a finished piece of work.
- Create, develop and realise a final outcome within the time available.
- Select, organise, prepare and display their personal confirmatory study in a professional manner.
- Evaluate their working methods and outcomes, identifying opportunities for additional development and improvement.

Assessment evidence will typically consist of:

- Records of negotiating and managing the project in an appropriate format, eg sketchbook, notes, personal reflective diary, records from tutorials and critiques.
- A significant body of work, eg research showing a range of ideas, developmental work, final outcomes.
- Supporting statement, eg written and illustrated, audio/video recording.'

Although the three stages are followed by all colleges, tutors have some discretion over the way in which students are taught. There are two main methods. Some colleges during the exploratory phase allocate periods of time to different art and design disciplines, perhaps one week spent on drawing, followed by others on graphics, fine art, fashion, photography and so on. Others prefer to set projects lasting several weeks, which require students to work in several disciplines at the same time.

Students often fall into the trap of assuming that Foundation courses are totally practical. They are not. At least half a day a week will be spent on contextual studies, including the history of art and design, and you will be expected to produce written assignments. This includes the creation of a personal statement (known as a 'statement of intent') that outlines, in no more than 500 words, your final major project. (WJEC students produce a 'personal review' instead of a statement of intent.)

Another common mistake is to think that studying on a Foundation course will be rather like being at school, with free periods during the day. Foundation course students work hard! Most courses will run from Monday to Friday, often from 9.30 to 4.30 or later. You can also expect to attend at least one evening class a week. Your working week will be divided into studio practice, lectures and seminars, visits and personal study time.

Although there are exceptions, Foundation courses are often very big, sometimes with as many as 400 students all following the same programme of study. For those of you used to small class sizes, this prospect can be daunting. In practice, nearly all students find that they quickly adjust to their new working environment. Many students find that they really feed off the hustle and bustle that comes with working in large groups and, in part, the course will be about learning to work with others.

You will find other differences:

- Don't expect lecturers to spend too much time chasing you up. Making the most of the course will be your responsibility. It will be up to you to attend.
- You will find yourself involved in group projects and can expect to forge strong friendships with your fellow students.
- The course will be exhausting at times but it will also be very exciting.

The build-up to the end-of-year show and the show itself are something that you won't forget.

Have a look at the views of a student and a course tutor. For examples of Foundation course artwork please see photo 2 in the colour section (between pp. 56 and 57).

| Charlotte Blower, Foundation course, Chelsea | 'I was surprised, when I first started the course, by the emphasis on self-motivation. There is more pressure on the students to push themselves, compared to school. No one forces us to do anything, so we need to create our own momentum. For this reason, the course suits those people who are really interested in art and are excited by it. What I like about the course is that it has opened my mind to art. At A level, we were restricted in what we could do, but here I have discovered much more about art, and the lack of boundaries in art, which makes it much more exciting. I have had a chance to experiment in lots of new areas such as fashion, textiles and 3-D. I have become particularly interested in graphics, and I am now applying for |

degree courses. My application for Foundation courses was a last-minute decision, but I now know that this is what I want to do. I chose Chelsea because I wanted to be in London to have access to as much art as possible. I liked Chelsea because it felt much more personal than some of the other colleges I looked at.'

Bill Watson, International Coordinator, Camberwell College of Arts (a college of the University of the Arts London)

'The Foundation course combines studio practice, group tutorials, lectures, museum visits, individual and group teaching. It is fast-moving. The students who gain most from a Foundation course are those with the most curiosity. They are the first in the studio in the morning and the last to leave. They participate in all the areas that the course has to offer. They are self-motivated, questioning, and do not allow themselves to be defined by the opinions of others. Their personalities will differ widely. They may be extrovert or introvert or all stages in between. They may recognise that a Foundation course is a journey of discovery and that the journey is guided by acts of looking, and they may also know that talent is not enough.'

CHOOSING A COURSE

1 | GETTING STARTED

You can do a first search on the internet. Have a look at the websites – the great thing about art schools' and colleges' websites is that they are extremely creative and entertaining. You can spend many happy hours investigating them. They are updated and changed on a regular basis but, at the time of writing, particularly good examples include the Edinburgh College of Art (www.eca.ac.uk), Norwich School of Art & Design (www.nsad.ac.uk), Birmingham Institute (www.biad.uce.ac.uk) and the University of the Arts London (www.arts.ac.uk).

Then get hold of as many prospectuses as you can and read them carefully. Don't just look at the pictures, but read about the course structure. If you love photography, and this doesn't seem to feature at a college you are considering, you ought to think twice about applying there.

2 | COURSE CONTENT

Look very carefully at exactly what you will be able to study. Consider the course content: Is it well structured? Is it flexible enough to allow for personal input? What about the range of subjects covered – is there a wide variety? Although Foundation courses are designed to allow you to gain experience across a whole range of disciplines, they do differ from college to college, and so it is important for you to choose a course that suits your needs. If your aim is to study fashion design at degree level, for example, then you will need to spend at least some of your time specialising in this area of study, so make sure that it is properly catered for.

3 | LOCATION

You can apply anywhere in the country for your Foundation course. However, the majority of students choose somewhere close to home, mostly for practical reasons. These include issues such as accommodation and living expenses, and the reassurance of knowing other people who are at (or have been at) the college. Cost is an issue since accommodation, food, travel and materials can be very expensive, and you will not get a student loan for a Foundation course. The courses are rated as further education rather than higher education. So – the downside is no loan. But there is a positive side to this. Students under 19 are not charged tuition fees in further education. This is worth taking into account, considering the amount you will have to pay for your subsequent course.

It is also worth remembering that Foundation courses are very demanding in terms of the time and energy that you will put into them. It is often hard to combine a Foundation course with a part-time job. However, many students do choose to move away from their local areas, either because the local college (if there is one) does not suit their preferences or because they are excited about moving to a new environment.

4 | FACILITIES

How big are the studios? Is the light good? What are the IT
facilities like? Does the college have a well-equipped
workshop in which you might experiment with a wide
variety of materials? Is there a photographic darkroom and
studio? Will you have access to a ceramics studio? What is
the library like? Is there a wide range of books? Does it
have a good multimedia section? Will you have to pay
studio fees, and if so what will they be? See page 28,
Chapter 2.

You should also think about other issues: What are the
communal facilities such as refectories, bars and social
areas like? Some colleges are attached to universities and
so you might be able to use their facilities as well.
However, this might also mean that the social facilities are
not on site and so some travelling may be necessary.

You will be able to answer some of these questions once
you have read the prospectus or looked at the website, but
many questions can only be answered by making a visit.

5 | OPEN DAYS, VISITS AND SPEAKER EVENINGS

It is vital to attend open days, or if this is not possible
because the dates clash with other commitments, to
arrange a private visit. The facilities and atmosphere of an
art college are the key to whether you will be able to
flourish there. Whatever the prospectus says, you will only
know whether a particular place is right for you by visiting
it. Try to talk to current or ex-students to see what they
think of the place. Look at the work that has been
produced. Does it excite you? Have a good look at the
studios. Check out the facilities – are they really as good as
they sound in the prospectus? See if the students are
working: a successful studio is one in which people are
working effectively – is that the case?

Many schools and sixth-form colleges organise speaker
evenings and other special events in which lecturers,
course directors and admissions tutors from local art
schools, ex-students and other specialists are invited to
talk about what to expect when you study Art at

institutions of further and higher education. Your local colleges may also offer a talk as part of their open day. Be smart and make sure that you go! Information straight from the horse's mouth can be extremely useful: you get the opportunity to evaluate not only what is being said but also who is saying it and how. Most visiting speakers will try to give you a flavour of the kind of work that you can expect to be involved with. Speakers are normally happy to answer your questions, may show you slides or give a PowerPoint display and will try to give you an overview of what is on offer. These seminars are extremely useful and are not to be missed.

6 | ATMOSPHERE

Visiting the college is so important because it is the only way to get a feel for its atmosphere. Most people who enjoy art find that the particular qualities of the physical environment and the ambience of the workspace are vital to their creative processes. This varies from person to person, so you won't find league tables ranking colleges in order of the inspirational effect that they have on their students. Some people like a 'buzz' around them – lots of noise, activity and excitement; others prefer a quieter, more contemplative environment. How will you know which colleges are right for you? The only way is visiting them and talking to students who are studying there. Never choose a college solely because someone else, such as a teacher or a parent, says that it would be right for you. Trust your own instincts about whether or not the atmosphere feels right. You are the one who will have to live there!

WHICH COLLEGE SHOULD I GO TO?

Even though Foundation courses now have a national framework, this may be interpreted very differently and what suits one student will not be right for another.

Using the six steps to choosing a course will have helped you to narrow your choice down to a handful of institutions. It is sometimes helpful to rank your shortlist in terms of location, facilities, the course, atmosphere, etc. You could give the top college in each category five points, the second four points, and so on. Once you have added up the scores, hopefully some clear winners will emerge. The important thing at this stage is to be honest with yourself about how the colleges match up to your requirements. If they don't fulfil your needs then even if going there 'feels' great, it won't be. Make sure that you stick to the criteria and try to establish a clear winner based on the facts. You may well find that a couple of colleges are equally suitable and, at that point, gut feeling may help you to make your decision, but as a general guide stick to facts and not fiction. In other words, don't believe the hype!

WORKING WITH YOUR TEACHERS

The final decision on where to go will be yours, but from time to time we can all benefit from a little guidance. Make sure that you work with your teachers. Talk to them. Ask them what they think your options might be. While no teacher is infallible, they will be able to help. Your teachers will probably have first-hand experience of local Foundation courses and will have some information about application deadlines and portfolio requirements. They will know which of the local courses are the most competitive – and whether you would be in with a chance. (Luckily, since there is no limit to the number of Foundation course applications you may make, you can still have a shot at the most difficult to enter while making one or more other applications for safety.)

In other words, teachers will know what is going on and how you are feeling. Talk to them and listen. It is highly likely that your Art teacher will be more closely involved with your application than any other person who teaches you, so make sure that you maintain a good relationship with them and try to take full advantage of their expertise.

'YEAR ZERO' COURSES

In Scotland, the usual system is for degree courses in Art and Design to be four years in length, with the first year being a diagnostic course – the equivalent of a Foundation course. Several institutions elsewhere in the UK are now also offering this pattern. If you like the idea of continuity

– no moving to a different university or college after Year One – you might like to look at the options. *There are important funding implications though. Year Zero students are enrolled on higher education programmes – which makes them liable for tuition fees. You can find further information on funding in Chapter 7.*

TOP TIPS

Get organised. You will need to open some kind of file to store all the forms and information you will receive. Make sure that you keep your diary or personal organiser up to date. If you don't use one, now is the time to start. Whether you use a sophisticated electronic organiser or a cheap diary from your local newsagent doesn't really matter. What does matter is that you organise yourself and stick to a manageable timetable. The last thing you want to do is miss out on the chance to visit a college because you forgot the date of the open day. Don't try to keep all of this information in your head – you won't be able to remember everything.

Before making your choice make sure that you also read the chapter 'How to apply'.

CHECKLIST

- ☐ **Send off for prospectuses**
- ☐ **Check out literature**
- ☐ **Check out websites**
- ☐ **Confirm dates for open days, visits and speaker evenings**
- ☐ **Draw up shortlists**
- ☐ **Talk things through**
- ☐ **Make a decision.**

2

Degree courses

This chapter provides an overview of degree courses in Art and Design. It aims to give you a feel for what you might expect at degree level and discusses aspects of how to find the right course for you.

WHERE ARE YOU NOW?

By the time Foundation students begin the second term of their course, most, though not all, have a fairly good idea of the direction in which their work is heading. Having completed the exploratory phase of the course in which you experimented with a variety of materials and methods across a broad range of different disciplines, you will have chosen a specialist area of study such as Fashion, Textiles, Painting, Illustration or Product Design. By this point you will have begun the process of putting together a portfolio and will be considering your options at degree level.

Alternatively, you may be a Vocational A level or Diploma student in your second year of study. In both cases, you will have begun to specialise in a particular area of Art and Design practice and will be considering your options at degree level. In some cases, although rarely, you will be in the A2 phase of your A levels and considering making a direct application to degree courses.

WHAT IS A DEGREE COURSE?

An Honours degree course is a specialist programme of study offering students the chance to develop practical skills in, and experience and understanding of, a specific area of art and design. Courses in Art and Design offered at degree level will combine practice with theory and, as such, most will require you to undertake some form of contextual studies alongside your practical work. This will vary from institution to institution and may consist of a formally presented illustrated dissertation or some type of multimedia presentation. All courses will show you how to operate within your chosen area of study at a highly sophisticated level.

Honours degree courses normally last for three years. Most of them are self-validating. (This means that the institutions offering them have the power to award their own degrees.) Some however – in smaller institutions – are awarded by a university which validates the course on behalf of the college. Do **not** worry if an institution does not award its own degrees! Some highly respected art schools which have international reputations and recruit students from all over the world do not do so.

Applications to most degree courses are made through the UCAS scheme.

Although there are exceptions, within the field of Art and Design there are three broad areas of study available at degree level: Fine Art, Visual Communications and Design, and the Applied Arts. It is from these three disciplines that you will select a specialist area of study. So, for example, Edinburgh College of Art offers a course in Furniture in its School of Design and Applied Art, leading to the award of a BA (Hons) Design and Applied Arts.

Specialisations found within the areas of Visual Communications and Design or the Applied Arts typically aim to prepare you for the workplace and, in that sense, may be highly vocational in nature. Sometimes they will include a period of work experience. Fine Art-based courses such as Painting or Sculpture will be more geared to professional studio practice (although your creative skills may also be valued by industry).

There are essentially four different types of degree you can choose to take: single or combined Honours, modular or sandwich degrees.

SINGLE HONOURS

Most Art and Design students studying at degree level in the United Kingdom follow this type of course. Competition for places at well-known universities and colleges is strong. Courses at colleges with international reputations (and there are many) attract enormous numbers of applications. Places at these institutions are as hard won as for any other type of undergraduate study! Courses typically run for three years and will require you to complete some form of moderated study of the history of art and design. You will have to pass this element of the course in order to be awarded your final degree.

COMBINED HONOURS

These courses make it possible to combine the study of distinct but often complementary subjects, for example Art and Psychology at Reading University.

MODULAR DEGREES

These courses enable students with a wide range of interests, including those outside the field of Art and Design, to combine the study of a variety of different subjects. At Oxford Brookes, for example, History of Art can be studied in combination with many other subjects (including languages, Accounting and Computing).

SANDWICH DEGREES

These are similar in style and content to single Honours courses and may be awarded as such, but will also contain some form of structured work experience. Most typically this will take the form of a 'year out' beginning at the end of the second year, in which you will work in industry, returning to complete your studies in the fourth and final year.

WHAT CAN I
EXPECT FROM
A DEGREE
COURSE?

Because you will be studying for three years or more and will be concentrating your efforts in a specific area of Art and Design, on a degree course you can expect to develop high levels of expertise. Degree courses should offer you excellent facilities and technical support within your chosen area and will also provide you with access to resources outside your specialisation, often by means of reciprocal arrangements with other institutions. You will be asked to consider issues and ideas at their most fundamental level and will be encouraged to fully realise your creative potential. For most students, studying becomes a way of life. You can expect to enjoy the full range of extracurricular activities that are available to all undergraduates.

Jason Michaels, BA (Hons) Fine Art Painting, Middlesex University

'My Foundation course was a lot of fun and I knew early on that I wanted to go on to do a degree, although it took a while before I was sure which area to specialise in. In the end I followed my instinct – I have always loved to paint. I knew London fairly well, having stayed with friends a couple of times, and was keen to move away from home.

'The course has been a real challenge. I didn't expect to be pushed so hard – I really had to think things through and talk to the other students and tutors about my ideas and opinions. I found this very difficult to begin with, but you get used to it eventually – we were all in it together.

'I knew from Foundation that I would have to work hard, but some aspects of the course surprised me. At school I hadn't really thought of myself as particularly academic and was dreading the written project. In fact I turned out to be pretty good at this sort of stuff! The social life was brilliant, although by the end of the second term I was exhausted. You really can't party all night and work all day.

'Taking a degree course was an excellent decision. I am a very different person from the one who started the course. My work has changed too. I intend to continue painting, but I also want to carry on writing as well. I have just written an exhibition review for my local paper.'

EDINBURGH COLLEGE OF ART – EXTRACTS FROM COURSE INTRODUCTIONS

BA (HONS) IN PAINTING

'The programme is designed to provide you with breadth of study and equips you with the technical skills in its initial stages, fostering your ability to organise your own programme of study and to work independently. Classes are timetabled and regular tuition and supervision are provided. In your second year you work in groups as you undertake various activities, while in third and fourth years you have an individual studio space. Throughout the programme, emphasis is placed on individual responsibility for study. Painting remains central to the activity of the School although you have the opportunity to explore your ideas through photography, video, printmaking and computer-generated imagery. The programme is intended to lead you towards the appropriate means of expression in the context of contemporary fine art practice.'

BA (HONS) IN SCULPTURE

'As well as a firm grounding in the technical processes involved in the discipline, students of sculpture at ECA are introduced to a wide variety of approaches to form, imagery and media as a means of developing creative ability and individual direction. Three separate aspects of the practice of drawing are taught. It is studied as a perceptual activity from life, nature and the environment, as a means of expression and as an adjunct to the making of sculpture and the development of sculptural ideas. Students are given workspaces in large shared studios, and the project-based programme is carried out in an atmosphere of close and continuing critical contact with staff.

'The liberal education in fine art provided by the Sculpture Department leads to a wide range of career opportunities. Many graduates go on to establish themselves in workshops and studios, and some become involved in teaching at all levels in the UK and abroad.'

BA (HONS) DESIGN AND APPLIED ARTS

FASHION

'Conceived as a practical as well as a creative introduction to the fashion industry, this programme offers a breadth of experience which students aspiring to a career in fashion will find invaluable. In addition to a comprehensive study of garment design, it develops an understanding of materials, cutting techniques, applied decoration and illustration. Collaborative projects with other ECA departments, such as Textiles, are also encouraged, offering a real opportunity to work alongside specialists in related fields.

'ECA has strong links with the fashion industry, and visits and placements throughout the course help students to build links with future contacts. Students from ECA have an excellent reputation within the industry, and the annual fashion show attracts attention from professionals and press alike. Some students also choose to follow their first degree with postgraduate work in the College.'

TYPES OF COURSE

There are an enormously wide variety of specialist courses available at degree level. Some disciplines will be familiar to you, others will be entirely new. Taking the three general areas of study already mentioned as a starting point, the following listings are designed to give an overview of some the courses available. These listings are not definitive – new courses are being set up every year. Please note that some specialist areas of study appear in more than one listing. This is because a subject such as Photography, for example, could be studied in the context of the Fine Arts, with an emphasis placed on personal self-expression, or might be offered as a Visual Communications course if it concentrates upon preparing you for a career in photojournalism.

CHOOSING A DEGREE COURSE

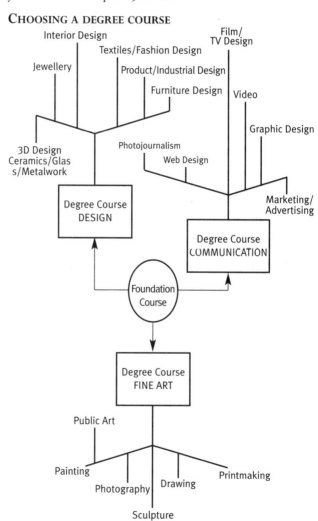

Below is a list of *some* of the courses available. It is by no means comprehensive. A list of all degree courses can be found on the UCAS website, in the 'course search' section, and in *Trotman's Green Guides: Art, Design and Performing Arts* — see 'Further information'.

FINE ART

These courses, which place an emphasis on personal creativity and self-expression, can cover a wide variety of disciplines and often include:

- Drawing
- Painting
- Photography
- Printmaking
- Sculpture
- Tapestry
- Textiles Studies.

For an example of a Fine Art studio please see photo 1 in the colour section (between pp. 56 and 57).

VISUAL COMMUNICATIONS

These courses are typically vocational and can sometimes include a period of work experience:

- Advertising
- Advertising and Editorial Photography
- Animation
- Biological Imaging
- Corporate Identity
- Film and Television
- Forensic Photography
- Graphic Design
- Graphic Design and Advertising
- Illustration
- Lettering
- Photography
- Print and Graphic Communication
- Public Art
- Typographic Design
- Visual Communication Design
- Wildlife Illustration.

For an example of a graphics show, please see photo 3 in the colour section (between pp. 56 and 57).

DESIGN AND THE APPLIED ARTS

Again these courses are normally vocational in nature and
as such will frequently aim to prepare you for professional
practice:

- Architectural Glass
- Ceramics
- Conservation
- Fashion
- Fashion Design with Technology
- Furniture
- Glass
- Interior Design
- Interior Textiles and Floor Coverings
- Jewellery
- Knitwear Design
- Museum and Exhibition Design
- Performance Costume
- Product Design
- Silversmithing
- Swimwear
- Textiles
- Theatre: Designing for Performance
- Transport Design.

For an example of a textile studio please see photo 5 in the
colour section (between pp. 56 and 57).

So far, we have been talking about Honours degrees, but a
new type of degree course is now available — which you
might like to consider.

**FOUNDATION
DEGREES**

Foundation degrees have been available since autumn
2001 and are on offer in a wide range of subjects. The title
is a little unfortunate where art and design are concerned –
since it could easily be confused with Foundation courses!
The new courses are a qualification in their own right and
can also lead on to an Honours degree course. Designed in
consultation with employers, they are courses that train
people in specialist career areas and develop:

- Work skills, relevant to a particular careers area
- Key skills, for example communication and problem solving
- General skills such as reasoning and professionalism.

If you do a Foundation degree you'll be able to choose between entering employment and continuing training in your job, or converting the qualification into an Honours degree through further study, usually by transfer into the second or third year of a related degree course.

Foundation degrees are available in a range of disciplines including Graphics, Fashion, Interior Design, 3D Design and Digital Media Design. A full list of courses and more information can be found in the Foundation degree section on the UCAS website (www.ucas.com).

FINDING THE RIGHT COURSE

1 | GETTING STARTED

Most students applying for places on specialist degree courses are either attending, or have been to, art school. Perhaps you have been studying close to home and want to move further afield, or maybe you are well established where you are and want to stay put. Probably you will have a pretty good idea of what you are looking for, but try to keep an open mind. Do your homework. Get hold of as many prospectuses as you can and read them carefully. Don't just look at the pictures, but read about the course structure and content. If you plan to study Furniture Design, for example, and love to make things in the workshop, make sure that the courses you are considering are supportive of this approach. Use the internet – the great thing about art schools' and colleges' websites is that they are extremely creative and entertaining.

2 | COURSE CONTENT

How will you know which course is going to suit you? For example, what is the difference between studying for a BA in Glass and in Architectural Glass? Degree courses in specific subjects will differ from college to college. Some Illustration courses, for instance, will place more emphasis on digital manipulation while others will focus more on traditional drawing techniques – so it is important for you to understand exactly what is being offered. Take full advantage of the literature available. Make sure that you read and fully comprehend the course specification. If you are unclear about anything, try to speak to the Course Director or Head of School. Look very carefully at exactly what will be studied, at what point in the course, for how long, and how much flexibility and choice you will have. For example, if you want to become a forensic photographer, make sure that you are not applying to a Fine Art photography course!

As many Art and Design graduates work as freelances it is important for them to understand how to run their own businesses – about finding premises to work in, tax and legal requirements, how to calculate costs when pricing their work – and how to market their work and present it to prospective employers or buyers. Ask now whether the course contains modules on self-employment, given either by course tutors or by the college or university careers service.

3 | LOCATION

You can apply anywhere in the country for your degree course. Consider the practicalities, such as the cost of accommodation and travel. Moving to a big city may be attractive but will you be able to afford it? Many students enjoy and benefit from the dynamism that city life can offer; some prefer to live and work in a quieter location. What will be right for you? For many students it is essential that they are close to galleries and museums. What are the local facilities like? Do they meet your needs?

Higher education is expensive and, although you may get some financial help, nearly all students have to raise funds privately. If you are planning to work part time, are there job opportunities?

4 | FACILITIES

Does the college have the facilities that you will need to study your subject? A degree-course studio should be very well equipped. Make sure that the relevant technology is up to date and kept that way. As well as working within your own field you may well need to cross over into other areas of art and design. Many art schools have reciprocal arrangements with other institutions. Do these exist and will they be practical? If, for example, you intend to study Sculpture, you will no doubt be looking for spacious, well-lit and well-equipped studios, but what about the IT facilities? Remember that you will have to put together some kind of contextual study. Are the computers up to the job and could you use them to create 'virtual' sculpture? As your skills develop so will your needs. Try asking yourself the question, 'Do I know what all the equipment is for?' If you do, then the course probably isn't well equipped.

You should also think about another issue: what are the communal facilities such as refectories, bars and social areas like? Some colleges are attached to universities and so you might be able to use their facilities as well. However, this might also mean that the social facilities are not on site and so some travelling may be necessary.

5 | STUDIO FEES
Most institutions charge students studio fees. These can vary considerably from place to place and, although they are hardly likely to influence your final decision when compared to other factors, it is worth finding out what they are and what facilities you get for the money. (This is not something that is usually quoted in prospectuses or course leaflets!) 'Studio fees' is a bit of a misnomer since it sometimes also includes course materials. It's also worth enquiring about prices of materials sold in the university or college shop, if this is the system that applies. You could check also –perhaps by asking a student on a visit day – if the final degree show involves students in much expenditure.

You will be able to answer some of these questions once you have read the prospectus or looked at the website, but many questions can only be answered by making a visit.

6 | OPEN DAYS AND VISITS
It is only by visiting a course that you will get a feel for its atmosphere. Most artists and designers find that the

physical environment and the ambience of the workspace are vital to their creative processes. This varies from person to person, so you won't find league tables ranking colleges in order of the inspirational effects that they have on their students. But ask yourself, 'What is the "vibe" like?' It might suit other people, but will it suit you? Make a point of talking to students who are studying there. Is the working environment a productive one? Can you picture yourself in it?

Never choose a college solely because someone else says that it would be right for you. Trust your own instincts about whether or not the atmosphere feels right. After all, you are the one who is going to study there!

7 | THE FINAL CHOICE

Remember you are going to have to live with this decision for three or four years, so try not to be carried away by a sudden rush of blood to the head. As important as trusting your instincts is using the steps outlined above to narrow down your choice to a handful of institutions. Go through this list and think things over carefully. Talk things through with those people who know you best – you will benefit from a second opinion. Rank your shortlist in terms of location, facilities, the course, atmosphere, etc. Try giving the top course in each category five points, the second four points, and so on. Use the scores to help identify which course meets your requirements. You will probably find that there are two or three courses that are 'up there'. Don't be afraid to trust your instincts, but make sure that your shortlist is based in reality and not fantasy.

David Bramston, Course Leader for the BA (Hons) Product Design course at the University of Lincoln

'We realise that students are taking a big and life-changing (not to mention expensive) step when they choose to enter higher education, and so when they come on a visit day we make sure that they see all our facilities. I also give a presentation about the course. We always invite them to bring a friend or relative with them to join them on the tour and the presentation.'

Sandy Farrell, Programme Leader of the HNC/D Fine Art, West Kent College (a partner college of the University of Greenwich)	'You need to start researching courses at least one year before you make the application. That gives you time to make visits. End-of-year shows are good because you can see students' work and get a feel for the place. If you can manage it, term-time visits are good too. Some places allow these. There is nothing so good as being able to talk to students who are already there.'
Stephen Brigdale, Senior Lecturer in Photography, Southampton Solent University	'It is not just the institution that is making a choice. Students are choosing too. They should be sure to see the facilities the university or college offers, including accommodation and student services, and establish that they would be happy there.'

Even choosing a Fine Art specialism is not as simple as it sounds. Tim Dunbar, who has worked in painting, sculpture and print – 'But I now call myself primarily a painter' – until recently acted as admissions tutor on Manchester Metropolitan University's Fine Art degree course. He says, 'The key thought when choosing a Fine Art course has to be "Which sort of Fine Art? Do I want to specialise in painting, printmaking or sculpture – and do so straight away – or would I prefer a generalist first year, leading to specialisation later?" Institutions offer different routes. There is no right or wrong way. Different approaches suit different students. It's horses for courses.'

CHECKLIST

- ☐ Send off for prospectuses
- ☐ Check out literature
- ☐ Check out websites
- ☐ Confirm dates for open days, visits and speaker evenings
- ☐ Talk to tutors
- ☐ Draw up shortlists
- ☐ Talk things through
- ☐ Make a decision.

3

POSTGRADUATE COURSES

Having completed your degree, you can continue
your studies, choosing from the wide variety of
postgraduate courses that are available.
Applications can be made either in the final year of
your degree or after you have graduated and
completed a period of professional practice.

TYPES OF
COURSE

When considering whether or not to apply for
postgraduate work your first choice will be between a
higher degree, diploma or certificate and between a taught
or research programme. Courses, which vary in structure,
include one-, two- and three-year postgraduate degrees,
leading to the award of an MA – or to a postgraduate
certificate that prepares students for specific professions,
such as a Postgraduate Certificate in Animation, a Diploma
in Museum Studies or a PGCE – the Postgraduate
Certificate in Education (the teaching qualification). You
will also be able to develop a career in research, with a
PhD or MPhil being the starting point.

MASTER'S DEGREES
Master's courses used to last for one year and the majority
were organised as taught programmes. However, there are
now numerous two-year courses. It is now also possible to
do a Master's degree by research – usually leading to a

Master of Philosophy (or MPhil). This is at a higher level than an MA but below that of a doctorate.

Taught Master's degrees usually take from nine to twelve months (or two years if you are a part-time student). The first six to nine months are normally studio and classroom based, and are followed by time spent on a research project.

DOCTORATES

PhDs (Doctor of Philosophy) are always achieved by research under the guidance of a supervisor – a member of academic staff who shares the student's interest and is expert in that particular area. Your area of study would be highly specialised and you would have to submit a thesis – of up to 100,000 words – based on original research. A PhD typically takes three years (but can take longer).

Courses cover the full range of Art and Design disciplines and, while it is usual to continue working within the same area of study that you have followed at undergraduate level, it is also possible to cross over into other areas.

Postgraduate courses are available at many colleges, art schools and universities. Many institutions offer courses at both undergraduate and postgraduate level, making it possible to remain within the same institution for all your studies. There are also specialist schools of art such as the Royal College of Art and the Royal Academy Schools of Art that offer only postgraduate courses.

APPLYING FOR A POSTGRADUATE COURSE

There is no centralised system like UCAS for postgraduate courses, nor is there a set closing date. Some taught programmes have deadlines, but it is often possible to begin a research programme at different points during the academic year. There may, in fact, be different starting dates throughout the year for all types of course – but the autumn term is still the most popular.

There is no limit to the number of applications that you may make, but most students make a maximum of six applications and on average around two to three.

Application procedures vary, but in the first instance you should refer to the college at which you intend to study. You will be required to submit a portfolio, attend an interview and, in some cases, present a formal proposal of an intended programme of study.

Funding for this type of course is often as hard won as the places gained on them. Once again, contacting the institution to which you are applying is a good way to begin exploring your options. Refer to 'Further information' at the end of this book.

4

CAREERS IN ART AND DESIGN

Every child is an artist. The problem is how to remain an artist once you grow up. Pablo Picasso

Wherever you are right now, take a look around you. Look closely at the environment you are in and think about the contribution made to your surroundings by artists and designers. Some may be obvious: there might be a painting on the wall, or you could take a look at the front cover of this book. If you are sitting on a chair, consider its design. Is it comfortable? If there is fabric covering the seat, what do you think of the colour and pattern? Look at the clothes you're wearing. Who was responsible for the cut and style? Who designed the fastening on your trousers? Where would you be without *that*? At home, consider the ergonomic design of your CD player and the cover design of the CDs that it plays. Think about the packaging of the food that you eat and the shapes of the cutlery that you eat with. Who took the fashion photographs in the magazine that you have just read? Who created the cover design? Who designed the logo? You may have done some research on art schools before reading this chapter – those websites were all designed by someone.

Artists and designers do not just exhibit their work in galleries and exhibitions. They are involved in almost all aspects of our day-to-day living. Artists and designers are concerned with how things look, feel and function. Virtually everything that is manufactured is designed to some extent. Most elements of the media – newspapers, magazines, television, websites, advertising – have considerable input from artists and designers. For every household name that emerges from art school to become rich and famous, there are many thousands of graduates who take up exciting careers that allow them to use their creative talents.

Most students who apply to Art and Design courses do so because they have a passion for art, and the ability to be creative. Some students say that their intention, after graduating, is to 'become an artist', by which they mean that they would like to use their creative skills in a way that is not manipulated by financial or corporate issues – perhaps they intend to have their own studio, to exhibit their work, and to become respected and admired by those who understand and value what they create. Realistically, however, not everyone has the talent, the focus, the energy or the luck to make a living in this way, and this is of course only one of the options available to those completing a course in Art and Design.

Perhaps a helpful approach when considering career options is to appreciate that the creative skills you possess are Key Skills. That is to say your ability to understand and communicate using visual language is as fundamental as being able to understand and use mathematics. Your talents will always be needed, especially when people are exploring new ideas. Landing on the moon was a great technological achievement: you can be sure that designers were involved every step of the way. Think about it – a footwear designer would have helped to design Neil Armstrong's space boots; perhaps they went on to work for Gucci! Looking at things in this way will help you to keep an open mind.

A reasonably high proportion of Art and Design graduates work on a freelance basis, or are self-employed. This can be extremely stimulating and satisfying because you can, to a certain extent, pick and choose the type of work that you wish to undertake. However, it can also be stressful at times because you will need to combine your creative expertise with your skills in business. For some, this is not always a good combination. Many medium- and large-sized companies employ full-time designers or artists. At the moment, the advertising industry (which employs a large number of Art graduates) is suffering a downturn, and work is becoming harder to find within this sector. However, very often when the economy is in a trough, it is advertising and related fields that bounce back first. Generally, employment rates for Art and Design graduates are pretty good, with about three-quarters of those looking for work finding it within a few months of graduating – although you need to bear in mind that for some this will mean involvement in short-term projects or contracts.

What do graduates do? (www.prospects.ac.uk), which is published annually, attempts to give a picture of what the graduates from one subject area in one particular year are doing. ('Attempts' because graduates are not very good at completing surveys!) The survey response from those graduating in Art and Design in 2004 – the latest year for which data are available – was actually a pretty creditable 82%. Information taken from the publication shows that:

- 14,465 students graduated in 2004 (11,730 were in the survey)
- 62.9% were in UK employment
- 1.3% were in overseas employment
- 3.7% were studying in the UK for higher degrees
- 2.0% were training to be teachers
- 2.4% were undertaking further study or training
- 10.3% were believed to be unemployed.

Of the 29.2% of people in employment related to their degree subjects:

- 8.4% as artists and commercial artists
- 4.1% were working as graphic designers
- 2.5% as clothing designers

- 2.4% as photographers
- 2.4% as industrial designers
- 2.0% as interior decoration designers
- 0.9% as web designers
- 0.9% as fine artists and general artists
- 0.8% as textile designers
- 7.6% 'others'.

Other Art and Design graduates were working in a variety of jobs, including marketing, sales, public relations, commercial and public-sector management, buying, retailing, catering and general administrative work. In other words, some were using their degrees as a generalist qualification; others were in temporary employment – just like graduates in other subjects.

A list of publications that provide information on careers and employment rates can be found at the end of this book in 'Further information'. Particularly useful publications are *Art and Design Uncovered* and *Careers in Art and Design*.

For the purpose of career options, degree courses can be divided into two categories: the Fine Arts and the Applied Arts. Examples of the first category include Painting, Drawing and Sculpture, and some Photography and Textile courses. The second category includes an enormous range of options, such as Communications, Fashion Design, Furniture Design, Art Restoration, Jewellery Design, TV and Film Design, Photojournalism and Architectural Photography. In many of these courses you will be developing skills specifically designed to help you meet employers' needs. If your degree falls into the second category then you may well find businesses that are looking for someone with your specific qualifications. However, as a Fine Arts student who, say, used digital manipulation techniques extensively in your work, you will be able to apply to companies that are as interested in your thorough understanding of that particular software program as they are in your ability to consider first principles. This ability to cross over demonstrates the value of Key Skills and will greatly increase your chances of having a successful working life.

The spider diagram will give you some idea of the variety of careers available within the fields of art and design. It is only intended to give you a sample of the options open to you.

CAREERS FOR ART GRADUATES

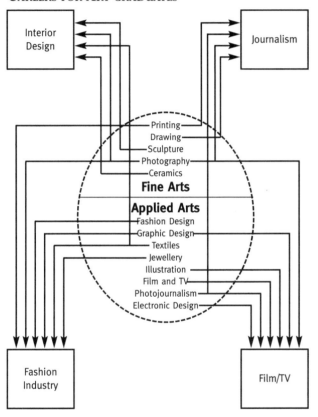

Overleaf is a list of some of the careers that you might consider. The list is not exhaustive.

Accessory Design
Animation
Architectural and Industrial
   Photography
Architectural Glass
Art Restoration
Art Therapy
Book Illustration
Carpet Design
Ceramics
Computer Games
Costume Design
Craft Design
Digital Imaging
Exhibition Design
Fashion Design
Fashion Photography
Film and Video
Glassblowing
Graphic Design
Interior Decoration

Jewellery
Journalism
Medical Illustration
Model Making
Museums and Galleries
Newspaper and Magazine
   Design
Packaging Design
Printmaking
Public Arts
Publishing
Sculpture
Surface Pattern Design
Tapestry
Teaching
Technical Illustration
Textile and Fabric Design
Theatre Design
Video and Film Production
Web Design

5

How to apply

This chapter explains the procedures for applying for Foundation, degree and HND courses. However, before you apply, you need to do lots of preparation. If you have not already done so, you should read the relevant sections on choosing a course (Foundation: page 5; Degree: page 17).

FOUNDATION COURSES

In most cases you apply directly to the art colleges for entry to their Foundation courses, and you can apply to a number of colleges simultaneously, since there is no central application scheme. There are some exceptions to this. For example, if you wish to apply for a place on a Foundation course at certain London institutions, you need to obtain a common application form from one of them, then send it to your first-choice college, naming a second choice as well. If your application to your first-choice college is unsuccessful, your application form is then passed on to the second choice. The courses are those held at the colleges that come under the umbrella of the University of the Arts London (Camberwell, Central Saint Martins, Chelsea, London College of Communication and London College of Fashion). From August 2006, Wimbledon College of Art will also become part of the University of the Arts.

The application forms vary from college to college. All require basic details about yourself and your education, but they differ in the amount of space (if any) that you have to write about yourself and your interests – the personal statement.

Unlike the UCAS scheme for applications to degree courses (see below), there is not one date by which all applications must be submitted. The closing date for applications varies from college to college, and so you must do your research early and make sure that you do not miss any deadlines. The closing date for applications is often the end of January, but this is not true for all colleges, so consult the prospectus or the website well in advance.

Most Foundation course applications need to be accompanied by a reference, usually from the head teacher or Head of Art at your school or college. If you are a mature student or are not studying Art at school, you should read the section for non-standard applicants (page 48). Warn the person you choose to do the reference well in advance that you are going to apply, and ask them whether they are willing to act as a referee. References normally take time to write, so do not surprise your referee with a form the day before the deadline. Even if he or she does manage to write it in time, it is less likely to be full of the necessary detail, and it will certainly not emphasise your planning and organisational skills!

Bear in mind that you are applying for a place on a practical course, and so the application form is only the starting point. The key elements of the selection process are the portfolio and/or the interview. Admissions staff will place most emphasis on evidence of high potential and creative ability. You should read the chapters 'Putting together your portfolio' and 'The interview' for more information. If your initial application is successful, you will be either asked to deliver (or send) your portfolio to the college so that it can be assessed by the selectors, or asked to attend an interview either at the same time as your portfolio is reviewed, or later.

DEGREE AND HND COURSES

If you are applying for degree courses, HND courses or Foundation degrees, you normally do so using the UCAS system. Almost all applications are made online using the UCAS 'Apply' system. Details can be found on the UCAS website (www.ucas.com).

If you submit a UCAS form, you always include a personal statement.

There are two ways to apply for Art and Design courses – Route A and Route B. If a course is listed as Route A in the UCAS handbook, you must use Route A to apply for it. If a course is listed as Route B, you must use Route B.

For courses using **Route A**, you can list up to six choices in the order that they appear in the *UCAS Directory*. Your application will be sent to each of the art schools at the same time. The form must be received by UCAS **by 15 January of the year that you wish to take up the place,** but you are advised to get your application in by mid-November so that the art schools can make arrangements to see your portfolio.

If you want to apply to the Fine Art course in Route A at the Ruskin School of Fine Art, Oxford, your form must reach UCAS **by 15 October**. You must also submit an Oxford application card by 15 October and a portfolio of artwork by 15 November. The addresses of UCAS and the Oxford Colleges Admissions are given at the end of this book.

For courses using **Route B**, you can list up to three choices in the order that they appear in the *UCAS Directory*. Forms must be received by UCAS **between 1 January and 24 March**, but you are advised to apply **by 8 March** if possible to avoid the last-minute rush. You must also fill in an interview preference form to indicate your first, second and third choices.

Your application form is then sent to your first choice, which will decide whether to invite you for an interview and then whether to make you an offer. If you decide to accept the offer, then UCAS will cancel your other choices. If you turn down the offer, or you do not receive an offer, your application form will be sent to your second choice, and so on. Route B applications will be sent to first-choice institutions from mid-February. If your form is received after this date, it will be sent to your first choice as soon as it has been processed.

You can apply for courses through both Route A and Route B, but you cannot choose more than three Route B courses. The following examples show the combinations of choices that are allowed:

3 Route B choices + 3 Route A choices
3 Route B choices + 2 Route A choices
3 Route B choices + 1 Route A choice
2 Route B choices + 4 Route A choices
1 Route B choice + 5 Route A choices

If you apply before 1 January for Route A courses, do not put down any Route B choices. If you want to apply for Route B courses, tick the box in section 3 on page 1 of the form showing that you want to apply for them later. You will be sent details nearer the time, and you will be able to change your personal statement and ask your referee to update your reference if you want to.

THE PERSONAL STATEMENT

If the colleges that you apply to require a personal statement (remember that applications submitted through UCAS always do) you need to plan this very carefully, as this will significantly affect your chances of either gaining an interview or being offered a place.

Some application forms only allow you to write a few lines to support your application, and they generally specify the information that they are looking for. For instance, the application form used by Hereford School of Art provides applicants with seven lines, and asks them to comment on their interests in art and design, how these have developed, and why they believe that the course is suitable for them. Clearly, with so little space available, your statement needs to be carefully planned. A good response might include a list of your particular interests, but you must make sure that they match the facilities that the college has to offer.

Many application forms give you enough space to write 200–300 words in support of your application. You should try to cover the following:

1 | Introduction – reasons for wanting to study art.
2 | Reasons for choice of college.
3 | Interests within art – areas of art that you enjoy, eg fine art, graphics.
4 | Influences – artists that inspire you, exhibitions that you have seen.
5 | Career plans or future areas of specialisation – if known.
6 | Other information – interests, work experience, travel.

Here is a sample personal statement:

I enjoyed Art at GCSE and decided to continue it at AS and A level. A level gave me the chance to experiment more, and to include ceramics and photography in my work. In my spare time I take evening classes in life drawing and always carry a small sketchbook with me so that I can make notes on things that inspire me. A Foundation course will give me the chance to investigate many new areas, such as graphics and design, and will help me to make the right choice for my degree course.

I would like to study at Melchester School of Art because I was impressed by the facilities, particularly the light and spacious studios. When I came to the open day, I met many current students and saw their work, and I felt inspired by what they had achieved in such a short time. Everyone that I met was very encouraging and enthusiastic, and I felt that I could be extremely motivated if I came to you. I also came to the graduate show and I hope to be able to follow a degree course here after the Foundation course.

I think that my major strengths are in drawing and painting, and I particularly enjoy abstract painting. At the moment, I am working on a piece I have called 'Woman', in which I am trying to bring out the essence of womanhood by using symbols and icons. I am also working on a self-portrait that combines photographs and acrylics, and on a female figure in the style of one of Matisse's Acrobats.

My favourite artists are Matisse and Antony Gormley. Some of my own AS pieces have been influenced by some of Matisse's later works, particularly his *Blue Nudes*. I went up to Gateshead to see Gormley's *Angel of the North* and then to Liverpool to see his sculptures in the sea. Recently, I went to see the Frida Kahlo exhibition at Tate Modern. I found her self-portraits very moving and I was fascinated by her use of symbols in her paintings. The contrasts between this exhibition, and Araki's photographs at the Barbican were extremely interesting. He also included references to himself in his photographs of women, sometimes in the form of symbols, and although his portrayal of women appears to be completely different from Kahlo's, there were many elements common to both artists' works.

I am not sure in which area of art my future lies, but at the moment I am interested in stage design and fabric design, although I have not had a chance to do this at school. However, last summer, I spent a week at our local theatre and was able to help the set designer work on the backdrops for a production of *The Tempest*.

Apart from visiting galleries and exhibitions, I enjoy music (I play the drums in a band, and have passed Grade 6 on the clarinet) and going to the cinema. This summer I am going to travel through Europe by train with some friends, and hope that this will give me inspiration for future work. My sketchbook will be with me all the way!

Notice that in the second paragraph, the applicant has mentioned that she went to an open day. Attending open days is important if you are to convince the admissions tutors that you are serious about your application. More information about open days is given on pages 12 and 28.

The best way to demonstrate your enthusiasm for art is to talk about your own work. This also gives the admissions staff an idea of your interests in a specific, rather than general, way. In the fourth paragraph, the applicant has mentioned some of her favourite artists. It is a good idea to try to include a contemporary artist, as you want to show the selectors that your interest in art is a developing one and that you are keen to be part of the current art scene rather than immersing yourself wholly in the past.

A word of warning: do not put things into the personal statement simply to impress the selectors. If you do get to the interview stage, you may be asked to talk about one or more of the artists that you have mentioned, and the surest way to be rejected is to be caught out. Notice, also, that the personal statement includes details of exhibitions that the applicant has visited, and what she found interesting in them. Never drop in the names of artists or galleries/exhibitions that you have visited without giving some indication of why they are important to you. The point of the personal statement is to demonstrate that you not only enjoy art in a practical sense, but you also think about it.

Another key element in the personal statement is the carrot that you dangle in front of the reader. In the third paragraph, the applicant describes, briefly, her own work but does not give much detail. She can be reasonably confident that, if she has an interview, she will be asked more about these pieces of work, and so she can prepare for this part of the interview in advance.

WHAT TO AVOID

The personal statement is just that, a statement that reflects your interests and influences: there are some things to avoid at all costs.

1 | You must avoid using very general statements that say nothing about you. 'I have always been interested in art, and get great enjoyment from my work', without an explanation or description of specific areas of interest or pieces of work, will not give the selectors anything to go on.

2 | Writing 'I would like to come to your college because of the facilities' is too general: say which facilities and why they attract you. Bring in your own areas of interest if possible.

3 | Never make any judgements about artists, their work, or exhibitions without backing them up: 'I went to see the Ori Gersht exhibition at the Photographers' Gallery, and I liked it' is not going to impress anyone. If, however, you added this it would demonstrate your own interest in the exhibition: 'because at first sight the images of landscapes seem peaceful and calming, but when you understand that this area was the site of many executions at the end of World War II and that members of his wife's family were amongst them, you appreciate the personal and private elements of his work. I also liked the way he overexposed the images using long exposures in order to make the photographic process more like that of painting.' Similarly, writing 'We were taken to see the Dan Flavin retrospective at the Hayward Gallery – I didn't like it' doesn't provide the reader with any information about you unless you explain why you didn't like his work.

SCOTTISH ART SCHOOLS AND COLLEGES

As already mentioned in the chapter on Foundation courses, the system in Scotland is slightly different: most degree courses are four years in length and incorporate the equivalent of a Foundation course. In some cases, students can enter the second year directly if they have undertaken a suitable Foundation or portfolio preparation course. For details, you should contact the institutions directly. In both cases, application is made through UCAS.

NON-STANDARD APPLICANTS

Not everyone who applies for Foundation courses is an A level (or equivalent) student. Similarly, some people apply for degree courses without having studied on a Foundation course. The main categories of 'non-standard' applicant are mature students (for FE and HE purposes, anyone over the age of 21) and overseas students. If you fall into one of these categories, you should make direct contact with the colleges that interest you to discuss your situation. The colleges' websites and prospectuses will also contain sections aimed at you.

It is important to be aware that, for all applicants, in addition to your personal qualities, the portfolio is the most important element in the application. Without a promising portfolio, you will not be offered a place. Make sure that you read the chapter 'Putting together your portfolio'.

MATURE STUDENTS
You may already have either a portfolio of work that you have done when you were at school (in which case, it will probably need updating), or perhaps a collection of pieces that you have been working on recently. It is often helpful to get guidance from art teachers, and for this reason many mature students will take evening classes, portfolio classes or Access courses before applying. (Sometimes this is best done at the college to which you intend to apply.)

NON-UCAS INSTITUTIONS
All Foundation course applications are made either directly to the institution or through a clearing system (for example, the London courses mentioned earlier in the chapter). In general, applications for degree courses are made through UCAS, but there are some exceptions. A list of non-UCAS institutions is at the back of the book on page 111.

Application to postgraduate courses is covered in Chapter 3.

OFFERS

FOUNDATION COURSES
In most cases you will receive an unconditional offer. In other words, the college has been convinced by your portfolio and interview, and they want you. All you have to

do then is to decide whether you want them! However, please note that in nearly all cases you will be expected to complete your current programme of study successfully.

CONDITIONAL OFFERS

Under some circumstances you might be made a conditional offer. This normally happens because the college feels that while your work is promising you are not yet ready to cope with the demands of a Foundation course, because they want to see further evidence of academic ability (you may be asked to achieve a particular grade at GCSE or A level in a subject), or because as an overseas student you would benefit from help with your language skills or with adapting to UK teaching methods in general. In this situation you may be asked to attend a summer course. (There is a charge for these courses.)

ACCEPTING AN OFFER

Since there is no centralised system for Foundation course applications (other than local schemes such as that run by the University of the Arts London) it is possible to hold a number of offers simultaneously. In this situation, the best strategy is to keep things simple, and not to try to juggle too many balls at one time. When you applied, you had probably already decided which college was your first choice, which was second, and so on. If you are lucky enough to get offers from a number of colleges, stick to your original plan and accept the offer from the place where you most want to study. Don't accept offers from everyone 'to keep my options open'. Talk to your teachers or careers advisers if you are unsure about your best course of action.

DEGREE COURSES

You may receive an offer direct from the art school to which you have applied, or if you are applying through UCAS you will (if all goes to plan) receive offers from more than one college. If you are lucky, these will be unconditional offers (which means that the offer does not depend on your achieving A level, AS level, GCSE or other grades).

CONDITIONAL OFFERS

If you receive a conditional offer, it will specify what the college requires of you – for instance, it may ask for a good grade in A level Art or, more commonly, good grades in other subjects, particularly if you are going to study for a combined Honours degree.

ACCEPTING AN OFFER

Once you have received all of your offers, you must decide which one you wish to accept as your firm acceptance (your first choice), and which (if any) to accept as your insurance offer.

If you have applied only for Route A courses, you can hold two offers: a firm choice (either conditional – CF, or unconditional – UF) and an insurance offer (either conditional – CI, or unconditional – UI).

If you have applied only for Route B courses, UCAS will send you a decision for your first choice. If it is an offer, you can either accept it or decline it. If you accept the offer, your other choices will not be considered. If you decline it, or the college or university does not make you an offer, your second choice will consider you, and so on. You will have seven working days to reply to a Route B offer. If you do not reply, the offer will be withdrawn and your next choice will consider you during the next round of interviews. If you have applied for Route B courses only, you can hold only one offer.

Here is a summary of the permitted combinations of offers:

Route A	Route B
UF	None
None	UF
CF + CI	None
CF + UI	None
CF	CI
CF	UI
CI	CF
UI	CF

CLEARING

If you are unsuccessful, either because you are not made any offers, or because you do not meet the conditions of your conditional offers, you are eligible to enter Clearing. The Clearing period begins in mid-August. This means that you can contact other colleges and make new applications. UCAS has also introduced a new system called UCAS Extra. This starts in March, and allows candidates who are not holding any offers to approach other art schools. For details of both, you should look at the UCAS website.

WHAT TO DO IF YOU DON'T GET AN OFFER

Three words: **don't give up**.

There are many options open to you. For degree applications, there are the Clearing and UCAS Extra systems (see above). For Foundation courses, you have the option of making direct contact with other colleges. You should also contact the colleges that rejected you to try to get their advice. It may be that they spotted a weakness in a particular area of your work and might be able to give you advice. If you can convince them that you desperately want to come to them and that you will work on that area – evening classes, for example – they might allow you to bring in your updated portfolio later on in the year for reassessment.

If all else fails, you could consider taking a gap year during which you can work on the portfolio to strengthen it. Many colleges offer portfolio courses specifically for this purpose.

SOME ADMISSIONS TUTORS' OBSERVATIONS

Dr Rhona Jackson, Head of Film, Television and Media Studies, University of Derby

'We have two degree programmes: Film and Television Studies (which is mainly academic, with some practical input), and Media Studies (which is mainly vocational). Both subjects can also be studied on a joint programme with another subject.

'We are looking for different types of student for the two courses. Film and Television Studies requires students who are prepared to read and think. Work is based on visual texts but they need to be able to apply theory to them. They must be prepared to read around the subject and apply what they have learned. Reading books is very important. Too many students these days use only the internet as a resource! They will be taught analytical concepts, then they must learn to apply them. We want students who are ready to do a close analysis of a visual text, then unpick it from different perspectives.

'Analysis is underpinned by reading. There must, therefore, be some evidence on the personal statement on the UCAS form that applicants do read around areas and that they do not think this course is simply about discussing films.

'Media Studies covers print (news, photography, the web) and broadcast media. Students write articles, make radio and TV programmes, write scripts, operate cameras and use an editing suite. Work is very hands-on, but they too are required to think. If they are intending to enter the media industries they need to be able to work independently. Employers all say that they require people who can think laterally, in addition to possessing practical skills. They also want people who can reflect on what they do and who are prepared to try to change things.

'In the personal statement, therefore, I am looking for evidence of motivation and enthusiasm. I'm also interested in anything that shows skill in time management. There are no exams on this course. Instead there is continuous assessment of coursework, essays and the products that students make. It's hard work on this course. The students find a 9am start comes as quite a shock! We all know that most of them these days have to have part-time jobs. If they already have a Saturday job I would like to know about it. That shows me that they are already balancing their time. Something in the reference saying that their attendance and punctuality are good is also useful!'

David Bramston, Course Leader for the BA (Hons) Product Design course at the University of Lincoln

'Our standard offer is 220 UCAS points or a profile of merits from A level and Diploma students respectively. Students come from all backgrounds – academic and applied A levels, Foundation courses and BTEC National Diplomas. We are keen on a mix of previous learning routes. The year group benefits from this.

'When I read the UCAS forms I look at the reference – but the most important section is the student's own personal statement. I read their comments carefully and make notes from these on possible topics to discuss at interview. They could write a little bit about their own favourite designers for example – BUT they must be prepared to discuss them later at interview. It is of no use to write a list of designers on the form and not be able to back up their interest in them!'

6

INTERNATIONAL STUDENTS

Students from all over the world come to the UK to study art or design courses. Many UK institutions are recognised internationally as being the best in the world. Last year, over 2000 overseas students gained places on art or design degree courses and many of these students will have followed Foundation courses in the UK for a year. If you want to be a fashion designer, an architect, a product designer, or if you want to train to work in the creative sides of TV, film, IT or advertising, studying in the UK will give you the best possible preparation and qualifications.

Most of the information contained in this book applies to international students as well as to home students. However, some aspects of the application procedures are different and if you are applying to study art or design at Foundation, degree or postgraduate level, you should be aware of these. The main differences are:

- Application deadlines
- Interviews
- Fees
- English language requirements.

APPLICATION
DEADLINES

You should read the information on application routes and deadlines contained elsewhere in this book. If you are applying for a Foundation course, you should also check the individual institutions' websites because deadlines vary from college to college. In some cases, international students from non-EU countries can apply for these courses later than UK or EU students, and the dates for interviews may also be later in the year.

For degree courses other than in art and design, the deadline for applications from non-EU students is 30 June. For art and design courses, Route A applications (see page 43) need to be submitted by 12 January. Any Route B applications received after 12 June will be automatically entered for Clearing. Further information can be found on the UCAS website.

INTERVIEWS

In order to be offered a place to study art or design at an art college or a university, someone from that institution will need to look at examples of your work. If you live in London, and you are applying to an art college in London, this process is easy: you turn up for an interview carrying your portfolio. During the interview, someone will look at your work and discuss it with you. If you live 8000 miles away, attending an interview is more of a problem.

Art colleges and universities approach this in a number of different ways:

- You send examples of your work by post.
- You scan your work and e-mail it.
- You are interviewed in your own country.
- You attend an approved course either organised by, or recognised by, the university.

Some institutions, such as the University of the Arts London, run portfolio preparation courses in a number of countries, successful completion of which will result in the offer of a place. Another option is a portfolio review session: the institution will organise events throughout the world where students can bring their work to be looked at

1 | *Fine Art studio, Norwich School of Art and Design.*

2 | *Foundation course projects, Norwich School of Art and Design.*

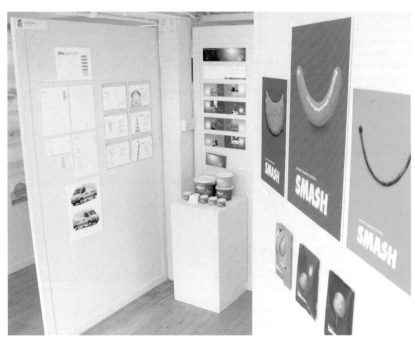

3 | *Graphics show, Norwich School of Art and Design.*

Every day is open day at Blackpool!

The School of Art and Design at Blackpool offers BA(Hons) Programmes, validated by Lancaster University, in Graphic Design, Photography, Information Illustration, Scientific and Natural History Illustration, Wildlife Photography, Fine Art: Professional Practice* and a Foundation Degree in Photography and Digital Design.

Come and visit on your own, with a friend or with your tutor. Whatever you decide, this is your chance to meet students and staff, tour the facilities and view student work. Alternatively, we'll see you at the London and Manchester UCAS fairs.

To arrange a time to visit us ring **Malcolm Pearson** on **01253 504442** or e-mail: **mp@blackpool.ac.uk**

For further information about the School of Art and Design or any of our courses, and to order a prospectus, visit our website: **www.art-design.blackpool.ac.uk**

* subject to validation by Lancaster University

School of Art and Design

Palatine Campus Palatine Road Blackpool
Lancashire FY1 4DW T : 01253 352352
F : 01253 291627 Minicom : 01253 355755

BLACKPOOL AND THE FYLDE COLLEGE
An Associate College of Lancaster University

LANCASTER
UNIVERSITY

4 | *End-of-year show, Norwich School of Art and Design.*

5 | *Textiles students, Norwich School of Art and Design.*

6 | *An applicant for the University of the Arts London with her portfolio.*

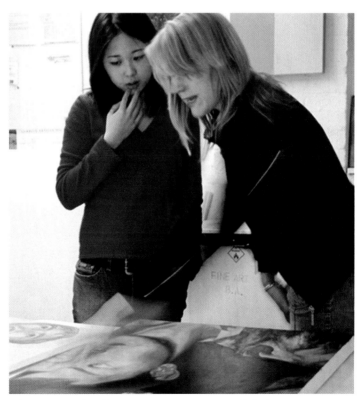

7 | *Critique and evaluation is an important part of the learning process at the University of the Arts London.*

8 | *Students discusses their portfolios at the interview.*

9 | *Student sketchbooks.*

Courses, placements, jobs — Huddersfield students excel

The University of Huddersfield offers undergraduate course in the following disciplines:

- Architecture
- Creative Imaging
- Design Business
- Fashion
- Fine Art
- Interior Design
- Multimedia
- Product and Transport Design
- Textile Design
- Textile Crafts

School of Art & Design Open Days every Wednesday at 11.00am

Set in the heart of the Pennines, the University of Huddersfield is justifiably proud of its top five position for graduate employment — a record based on quality academic achievement and our industry contacts. Our sandwich courses give you a full year working in your chosen field. Companies as far afield as New York or Hong Kong welcome students from Huddersfield.

The University campus is set in the centre of Huddersfield which has a friendly and supportive community with easy access to the cities of Leeds, Sheffield and Manchester.

You are welcome to visit the School of Art & Design every Wednesday between 11.00am by appointment or on the University Open Days on 21 June, 16 September or 25 October 2006. To book a visit to the School of Art & Design please call 01484 473813.

School of Art & Design
University of Huddersfield
Queensgate, Huddersfield HD1 3DH

Tel: +44 0 1484 472281
Fax: +44 0 1484 472 940
www.hud.ac.uk

University of
HUDDERSFIELD

10 | *Student sketchbooks.*

11 | *Student sketchbooks.*

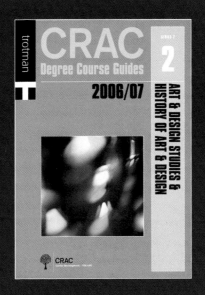

trotman

trotman

CRAC
Degree Course Guides

2006/07

2

ART & DESIGN STUDIES & HISTORY OF ART & DESIGN

CRAC

Find your ideal degree with this guide. It tells you how each university teaches art & design so that you can find the course matching your interests and abilities.

Covers: fine art, graphic design, photography, imaging & time-based media, textiles, fashion, 3-D design, multidisciplinary art & design and history of art & design.

ISBN: 1 84455 058 3
£9.99

For more information and to order:
call 0870 900 2665 or visit www.trotman.co.uk

new edition

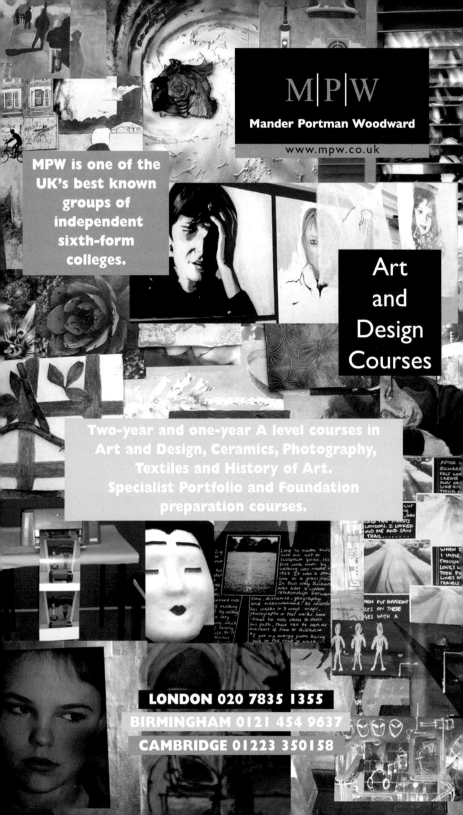

M|P|W
Mander Portman Woodward
www.mpw.co.uk

MPW is one of the UK's best known groups of independent sixth-form colleges.

Art and Design Courses

Two-year and one-year A level courses in Art and Design, Ceramics, Photography, Textiles and History of Art. Specialist Portfolio and Foundation preparation courses.

LONDON 020 7835 1355
BIRMINGHAM 0121 454 9637
CAMBRIDGE 01223 350158

DIPLOMA · DEGREE
POST-GRADUATE

City & Guilds of London Art School

FINE ART
BA (Hons) & MA Fine Art Painting & Sculpture
CONSERVATION
BA (Hons) & Post Graduate Diploma Conservation Studies
HISTORIC CARVING
Diploma & Post Graduate Diploma
Architectural Stonecarving · Ornamental Woodcarving
FOUNDATION COURSE Art & Design
PART TIME Drawing · Printmaking · Stone/Wood Carving · Gilding

All applications should be made directly to the school - we do not recruit through UCAS

http://www.cityandguildsartschool.ac.uk

124 Kennington Park Road London SE11 4DJ Tel: 020 7735 2306 Fax: 020 7582 5361 e-mail:info@cityandguildsartschool.ac.uk

trotman

Everything you need to
know to make your money
go further at university.

ISBN: 1 84455 075 3
£14.99

For more information and
to order: call 0870 900 2665
or visit www.trotman.co.uk

new edition

BA (Hons) in Contemporary Applied Arts*,
Fine Art*, Graphic Design*, Multimedia Design and
Digital Animation*, Photography*, Surface Design
Foundation degrees in Ceramics, Contemporary
Jewellery, Drawing, Graphic Design and Furniture Crafts
Diploma in Foundation Studies (Art and Design)

Institute of the Arts

Brampton Road, Carlisle, Cumbria, CA3 9AY
0845 6076563 info@cumbria.ac.uk www.cumbria.ac.u

and discussed with teachers. Details of these courses and events can be found on the institutions' websites, and are also advertised locally.

Under some circumstances (for example, if you are considered to be too young for direct entry onto a Foundation course, or if your English is not sufficiently good) you may be advised to spend a year on a pre-Foundation course at a recommended school or college in the UK before proceeding on to the Foundation course.

Robert Green, Manager of International Student Support, University of the Arts London

'The majority of our courses at the University of the Arts London are studio/practice-focused and as such entry is generally based on portfolio assessment and interview. Therefore, careful preparation and selection of the portfolio is an essential preliminary to the interview.

'The portfolio is a visual diary. It is the documentation of the individual's journey, both perceptually and conceptually, over a period of time. In essence the portfolio should be comprehensive, demonstrating a breadth and depth of inquiry, curiosity and genuine investigation. Solid practical skills and experience of working with a variety of media and techniques are, in addition, of equal importance.

'The portfolio should include work done in school or college and at home. The range of approaches and the materials used should show that the applicant has made the most of the opportunities around them, both in terms of what they are being taught and the art room or studio facilities that are available. We particularly look for evidence that an applicant has been prepared to develop some ideas further on their own initiative and in their own time.

'Time and care is needed in selecting the portfolio, and systematic decisions about what to include and

how to organise and present the work should be
made. Obvious repetition should be avoided, as
should over-selection. A limited number of relevant
works in progress may be included because, first
and foremost, we are looking for potential.

'Ideally, a portfolio should consist of between 25
and 50 pieces of recent work, completed over a two-
year period. This collection of work should show
evidence of a broad-based creativity and include
sketchbooks, visual research books, idea sheets and
any experiments or explorations in three
dimensions. The portfolio should demonstrate,
through project and thematically based work,
evidence of individual creativity and the
development of ideas. Generally, it is important that
work reflects and demonstrates creative thinking
and a personal commitment to a particular project.

'In the early stages of all our courses we concentrate
on combining technical workshops with set
projects. As courses progress, assignments generally
become more wide-ranging and contextually based.
All practical work is undertaken within a
framework of individual and group tutorials as well
as studio criticism sessions, where all students are
encouraged to offer constructive critical opinions
and advice to each other. Critical exchange and
dialogue is central to our teaching approach.
Therefore, at interview, all applicants are expected
to discuss and evaluate the development and
context of their work so as to demonstrate broad
understanding and ability to think critically.

'A portfolio does not supplement an interview, but
is the main factor in assessing a student's future
potential. Thus the portfolio is even more essential
to students who are unable to be interviewed.

'You should present your portfolio in the form of
colour photographs, colour photocopies, slides or
CD. It is best not to send originals in the post. You

should send between 25 and 50 pieces of work. The portfolio should ideally be approximately A4 size if being sent by post.

'University of the Arts London have representatives in a number of countries across the world. Our representatives can assist with all aspects of the application procedure, offer information about programmes and courses and assist with immigration matters.

'When our senior academics make their next scheduled visit, a local representative can arrange for applicants to have an interview or an advice session with an academic. Our contact details and an overseas schedule can be found on our website.'

FEES

The fees for Foundation courses for non-EU students are between £6000 and £7000. For degree courses, they are likely to be between £9000 and £10,000 per year. Living costs could add an extra £8000–£10,000 a year. Postgraduate courses can sometimes be less expensive than degree courses. You should check the institutions' websites for more information. Further information on fees and funding can be found on the UKCOSA website. The address is given at the end of this book.

ENGLISH LANGUAGE REQUIREMENTS

You should refer to the individual institutions for their requirements. To give you an idea of what level of English is required, the University of the Arts London gives this advice:

'The ability to understand, communicate and learn in English is an important requirement for acceptance into University of the Arts London. If English is not your first language or primary language, you must provide us with evidence of your English-language ability (such as an IELTS score and certificate).

'You can apply before you have the required level of English language ability. The requirements for entrance to full-time courses are shown below:

- Fashion Portfolio: IELTS 4.5
- Foundation Studies, Diploma, Access and ABC Diploma courses: IELTS 5.0
- Foundation Degree Award: IELTS 6.0
- Bachelor of Arts/Graduate Certificate/Graduate Diploma: IELTS 6.5
- Master of Arts: IELTS 7.0.'

7

FUNDING

FOUNDATION COURSES

Foundation courses are classed as further education (FE) courses, rather than higher education (HE). For this reason, student loans are not available. However, students from the UK or the European Union who are under 19 on 31 August in the year that the course starts are eligible for free admission. Students who do not come into this category will have to pay tuition fees, which are likely to be about £800–£900 per year for UK/EU students and £6000–£7000 for international students.

DEGREE AND HND COURSES

All UK and EU students pay tuition fees of up to £3000 per year as a contribution towards the cost of the course. The money does not have to be paid whilst you are studying – you can take out a loan which does not have to repaid until you are working and earning more than £15,000 per year. Some students will have up to 100% of this paid by their local authority, depending on the income of their parents. Details of how these grants are calculated can be found at www.dfes.gov.uk/studentsupport. Scottish students who choose a Scottish university or art college do not pay any tuition fees, but instead pay a *Graduate Endowment* after they graduate. At the moment, the Graduate Endowment is about £2000. Welsh students studying in Wales will be charged up to £3000 a year, but will receive a grant (non-repayable) of up to £1800 per year to offset the fees. The UCAS website has full details of fees and support arrangements.

Students on HE courses are eligible to apply for student loans to help with living costs. Students can borrow up to about £5000 per year.

POSTGRADUATE COURSES

There is no automatic right to funding or student loans for this type of course. Students are often self-funding – or may be assisted by scholarships from universities or from other organisations. Contacting the institution to which you are applying is a good way to begin exploring your options. Refer to 'Further information' at the end of the book.

OTHER SOURCES OF FUNDING

Commercial organisations, charitable trusts, educational institutions and government agencies all offer sponsorship, special grants, access funds and scholarships, but these sources of finance are limited and hard to come by. If you are facing financial difficulties, a good place to start looking for information is the college that you are applying to.

Contact details for the Student Loans Company (SLC) and for organisations that provide further information on student finance can be found in 'Further information' at the end of the book.

PUTTING TOGETHER YOUR PORTFOLIO

For most students making the move into higher education, the offer of a place is normally made on the basis of past academic performance, personal statements and references, predicted grades for forthcoming examinations and, increasingly, an interview. With art school applicants, all of the above applies but with one very important addition: you will need to show the college your work. Whatever the particular format your interview may take (discussed in the next chapter), put simply, you will turn up with your work, the college will look at it and you will get the chance to talk about your work, yourself, and also ask and answer questions.

For some of you this may seem a daunting prospect. Most artists worry about showing their work to others. It's not surprising when you think about it. Having put our heart and soul into what we do, naturally we worry about negative judgements, particularly from people who really don't know much about art in the first place. Don't panic! Attending an interview with a portfolio of your work gives you a big advantage. Unlike your contemporaries who rarely get the chance to show what they can do except in exams, not only do you get to show what you are best at – being creative – but you get plenty of time to prepare in advance, will have a good idea of what to expect, and all the people interviewing you will be artists themselves so they will understand what you are doing.

WHAT IS A PORTFOLIO FOR?

All of the colleges that you apply to will be interested in your qualifications, references and experience, but above all they will be concerned with who you are, what you have done and what your potential is. Demonstrating these things is the function of the portfolio.

WHAT IS A PORTFOLIO?

Quite literally, a portfolio is a folder containing examples of art and design work. Professional artists and designers take theirs to job interviews. You will show your portfolio to the admissions tutors of the courses to which you apply. Portfolios come in all shapes and sizes and in many cases you will be able to use the same portfolio (normally A1 size) in which to display your work for both Foundation and degree course applications. There are some exceptions. For example, a student applying for a specialist degree course in Photography might choose to use a portfolio specifically designed for that purpose. They are often smaller and are sometimes referred to as a 'book'. Equally, the term 'portfolio' can be used to describe any collection of works for presentation even if they are not actually displayed exclusively in a folder.

WHICH PORTFOLIO SHOULD I BUY?

At this stage don't buy one at all. Wait until you have read the whole of this book, have had a chance to think things over and, most importantly, have some idea of what you are going to put in it. As a guide, buy the best one that you can afford. Look at the quality of the zip if it has one and check that the ring binder works well. Is the handle strong and comfortable? When thinking about sizes, consider how big your work is. Don't bite off more than you can chew. If you can't carry it, it's too big! Above all, remember that it is the quality of your work that counts and not the quality of the thing that you carry it in.

The following guidelines apply to portfolios for both Foundation and degree-course applications. Read them carefully: they describe the qualities that you should look for in your work and will help you make decisions about which pieces to select. Later in this chapter there are also sections giving guidance on the requirements for each type of portfolio. Make sure you read the contributions made by course tutors.

GETTING YOUR WORK TOGETHER

The first step in putting together your portfolio is to gather together all of your work. When you do this it might be tempting to say, 'I won't need that' or, 'That's no good', but at this stage just concentrate on getting all of your work in one place so you can see what you've got: finished pieces, unfinished pieces, sketchbooks, models, notebooks, written work, old work, new work – get everything! This is important because not only will you find things that have been tucked away that are actually very good, but also as you look through your work you will begin to see relationships emerging between new and old pieces. A small sketch that at first may seem rather unimpressive might have inspired a later, much more accomplished piece. The ability to make judgements and to evaluate what you have done, to recognise a good idea and to develop it further, is an important part of the creative process. Admissions tutors will be assessing to what extent you are able to do these things.

It may help you to organise your work into categories: the following list will provide you with a starting point:

- finished pieces
- works in progress
- drawings from observation
- drawings of invention
- life drawing
- sketches and studies
- models and maquettes
- sketchbook/journals
- contextual studies/written work.

THE IMPORTANCE OF DRAWING

Albert Einstein used the formula $E = mc^2$ to express his famous theory. Scientists use mathematics to express and explore their understanding of the world and how it works. Artists and designers do this with drawing.

Drawing could usefully be described as the act of making marks to convey meaning. Artists and designers use drawing to record observations, work out ideas, pass on information, express feelings and emotions and resolve practical problems. Drawings are often used to help us visualise how things fit together. For example, scale drawing can be used to work out if all the units of a kitchen will fit into the space available. Diagrams and flow charts can be used to demonstrate how ideas and principles relate to each other. Drawings come in all shapes and sizes and are made with a variety of different purposes in mind. Examples of types of drawing include:

- life drawing
- observational drawings such as those done from a still life or made in the field (eg architectural details)
- plans and designs
- sketches and drafts.

Whichever course you apply to will want to see your drawings in one form or another because they are evidence of your visual intelligence. Your drawings demonstrate that you can perceive, understand, invent and communicate visually. These abilities are at the core of successful art making.

SKETCHBOOKS

Sketchbooks fulfil many purposes. They are a place in which artists and designers begin the creative process. They are also a place in which to store cuttings, postcards and virtually any other articles that will fit. They are the place in which you can put your ideas, thoughts and feelings down on paper. Typically, interesting sketchbooks contain visualisations of many different types, made by you for a variety of different reasons.

These images might take the form of carefully studied observational drawings or quick sketches or doodles. In a sketchbook you will refer back to previous ideas and make relationships between images on one page and those on another. Perhaps you have spent some time experimenting with different ways of making marks. You will be familiar with many of the effects that you can get with a pencil, but what kind of drawings could you make with a nail? A sketchbook or journal is the place where you might try something like this. Maybe you have been using your sketchbook to work out the volume of a space so you can calculate how much concrete you would need to fill it? Why would you want to know? At this stage you are probably not completely sure and you don't need to be. The sketchbook is a place where you can try things out even if they seem crazy; it will reveal the extent of your curiosity. In this sense, sketchbooks can be highly personal and frequently become much cherished. They also provide evidence of your creative development because they are time-based.

With very few exceptions, all courses will want to see your sketchbook work. For examples of student sketchbooks please see photos 9–11 in the colour section (between pp. 56 and 57).

PROJECT WORK

The ability to undertake and complete a project, whether it is self-determined or in response to a set brief, is one of the qualities that prospective art schools and colleges will be looking for. Work developed over an extended period, formed by experimentation, contemplation, reflection and risk taking, says a great deal about its creators. Are you willing to stick with something to the end? Will you test a theory to the point of destruction? Can you keep an open mind? A project piece will demonstrate your imagination, invention and skill and give evidence of your willingness to condense your theories and commit to a final outcome. If it has been made as part of a group project it will also show your ability to work with others. Normally this project work will have been completed on your current course of study and will show to what extent you have taken advantage of the training and support you have been given. These pieces might be two- or three-dimensional or time-based and may use a variety of different media.

It can also be very helpful to include some work in progress. Unfinished pieces can have a freshness and ambiguity that often stimulates conversation. Overly prepared portfolios in which everything is polished to perfection feel stifled and dishonest. Including an unfinished piece or two will help to avoid this problem.

PERSONAL WORK

Most artists and designers have a strong desire to be creative. Whether they are extrovert or introvert by nature, creative people have a need to express themselves. Inevitably, this does not stop when we leave the classroom or studio. Personal work may take a variety of different forms, but its essential qualities are that you did it because you wanted to, it contains your own opinions, thoughts and feelings, and was made to fulfil your needs. Maybe you feel strongly about something and want to make a point, or perhaps you are in a band, have recorded a demo and need a CD cover. In both cases, you would naturally have a need to create. Personal work says a lot about who you are and demonstrates your passion and commitment.

CONTEXTUAL STUDIES / WRITTEN WORK

Written work is often overlooked at interview but should be included if possible. At degree level it will be a requirement to complete some form of contextual study, and on a Foundation course you can expect to be fully engaged in critical thinking (although you probably will not be required to produce an extended written piece). Reflecting upon the work of others and responding to its qualities is a fundamental part of the creative process. This work will give you the chance to demonstrate your ability to explore ideas and concepts, learn from the work of others and, in many cases, will show how you are able to make choices about typefaces, justifying text and formatting illustrations.

MATCHING YOUR PORTFOLIO TO THE COURSE SPECIFICATION

Make sure that you read the course's portfolio specification thoroughly. Talk things through to make sure that you are clear about what is required. Each course will have its own requirements. For example, many courses ask you to limit your portfolio to a particular number of pieces. Whatever the requirements are, respect them: they will be there for a reason and are your best guide to what to include. In many cases it will be necessary for you to adapt your portfolio for each course to which you apply. Make sure that you give yourself time to do this.

SPECIAL CONSIDERATIONS

It may not be possible to take all of your work to the interview; perhaps it is too big or too fragile. For practical reasons, art schools and colleges inevitably have to put some restrictions on what can be accepted. If this is the case, in most instances it is perfectly acceptable to take slides or photographs, but do check with the admissions tutor first. It is always preferable to take the original work if possible, and if you do take photographs make sure that they are good ones.

LABEL YOUR PORTFOLIO

Make sure that you clearly identify your work. You do not want there to be any confusion about who did it and you want to make sure that you will get it back. This is particularly important if you have to submit your portfolio in advance of the interview – make sure that you put your name and address in an obvious place.

ENROLLING ON EVENING COURSES

Evening courses can be a valuable source of extra tuition. They give you a taster of what being at art school is like and can be a lot of fun. For mature applicants, they provide the opportunity to work with teachers and become reacquainted with a teaching environment. If you don't have access to a life model, for example, consider taking life-drawing classes. Courses could be theoretical in nature and could cross over into other disciplines that are new to you, for example animation. Not only will this help to build up your portfolio, but it will also be an excellent demonstration of your commitment.

PORTFOLIO REVIEWS

Many schools and colleges offer portfolio review sessions, sometimes leading up to mock interviews. Certainly your teacher or tutor will offer you advice and support.

Set specific goals such as 'I need more life drawing', etc. We are not always the best judge of what to put in and what to leave out of our portfolios. You are going to need a second opinion, and taking the advice of an experienced teacher will help enormously.

FREAK-OUTS

Most artists feel overwhelmed from time to time – it often goes with the territory for those of us who are willing to test things to the limit. The process of putting together a portfolio can feel stressful for some. Why is this? The main reason is that the student is poorly prepared and leaves everything to the last minute. This can be disastrous.

I met a group of A level students applying to art school and asked them the following question: 'If you could give a fellow art school applicant one piece of advice on how to put together a portfolio, what would it be?' Their unanimous response was: 'Start early!' They all shouted it! Setting manageable weekly deadlines and keeping an honest record of what you have and have not done will help enormously. Not convinced? Read on.

Caroline

'I was still preparing my portfolio on the day of submission!

I arrived two hours late! Fortunately the college agreed to accept my work, liked it and I was subsequently offered an interview. I was very, very lucky. It was a day I never want to go through again. It was a nightmare!'

Jerome

'As an A level Art student, there were a lot of things I should have done to prepare which I didn't. What I didn't do was consider going to art college early enough. I applied in January but I didn't really start researching into art colleges until the month before. Because of this I was late in starting to put my portfolio together. Fortunately, I had regularly attended life-drawing classes so I had plenty of drawings to choose from, but if I hadn't, there would not have been much time to do anything about it. I have still got a lot to do and my interview is only a couple of weeks away. I really wish I had started earlier.'

Monica

Monica came from Korea and spent a year in London studying A levels in Art and Photography. She had been interviewed in Korea by the University of the Arts London, who recommended the A level route. Her interviewer was impressed by her portfolio, but felt that it lacked variety. Monica was 16 years old when she was interviewed, and would have been too young to start a Foundation course at the university. Monica says: 'At the time, I was disappointed not to be going directly to the university. However, the one-year A level courses I took gave me a chance to experiment with new techniques and to gain confidence. I got two A grades and this made me feel much more sure of my own abilities when I started my Foundation course.'

Kay

Kay attended several interviews for Foundation courses. 'There was a lot of variation in the interviews I attended. At one art college, we discussed our work in small groups and so we were able to see what other students had brought along. This was a bit intimidating as some of them had produced amazing things. At another college, I was interviewed on my own, and was able to discuss my work with one of the teachers from the college. Although I was put on the spot a bit more, I preferred this because I felt more at ease talking without an audience!'

Jenny 'If I had to give prospective students one piece of advice, it would be to practise talking about their work with their teachers before going to the interview. Talking about your own work is difficult even when you know the person you are talking to, and in an interview it is very stressful unless you have practised beforehand. I felt such a phoney when I was talking about why I had created the pieces in my portfolio the first time I did it, but it got easier the more I did it. My A level teachers at my college helped me by organising mock interviews before the real thing.'

PORTFOLIO FOR A FOUNDATION COURSE

This should contain as wide a variety of work as possible. You may think that you are heading for a career in fashion design, but you are applying for a diagnostic course that aims to confirm that choice for you or point you in another direction. Tutors want to see potential in all sorts of areas, so include:

- drawings and paintings made from observation and imagination, using a variety of media
- life drawings
- project work made on your current course and for yourself
- sketchbooks
- colour work made in a variety of media
- examples of design work and model-making
- printmaking
- photography
- multimedia work such as video
- contextual studies or written work
- photographs of three-dimensional work if it is not possible to transport it.

Don't worry if you can't include all of these; very few students are able to. Remember that admissions tutors will primarily be looking for potential and motivation.

SOME ADMISSIONS TUTORS' GUIDANCE

FOUNDATION COURSES

Roy Naylor, Head of the Foundation course at Winchester School of Art at Southampton University

'What should be included in a portfolio? We want creative individuals so we do not prescribe what should be included. This is a diagnostic course; students are not expected to have concentrated on one aspect at this stage, so work in all or any media can be included. We are looking for real interest and passion. I would say, "If in doubt, don't leave it out!" We know the focus of most of our local schools very well and know that some concentrate on fine art or textiles. This does not matter because we want to see examples of work done by students in their own time as well – and also expect to see their sketchbooks and notebooks. We are looking for evidence of future potential rather than for any kind of past experience or knowledge.'

Bill Watson, International Coordinator, Camberwell College of Arts (a college of the University of the Arts London)

'A portfolio is essentially a well-presented collection of a student's visual work. Portfolios may vary in size, shape and number of works included, but broadly should demonstrate visual skills alongside imagination, invention and a personal approach to ideas and concepts. All the work need not be "finished". Interviewers are interested in the creative process. What was the idea? How was it researched and developed? Were a single or many resolutions possible? The sketchbook or workbook is important in this process. It can reveal visual thinking alongside written notation. In interviewing, many reviewers find a student's potential is evident in the sketches, doodles, scratching, half-formed ideas and cartoons of a sketchbook. A "finished" work may say one thing but a workbook says many.

'If paintings or sculptures are included, how did they come into being? Was their source from the visual world – a museum, gallery or public event? Or was it from the studio – a life drawing or still life? Did it arrive from a memory, photograph, a written text or a piece of music? Can the portfolio show the development and growth of a visual idea?'

PORTFOLIOS FOR SPECIALIST COURSES

While this portfolio should contain a range of work demonstrating your all-round ability, you will obviously need to demonstrate a commitment to a particular area of study and show a level of skill and ability in that field. However, admissions tutors will be realistic about the extent to which you will have been able to develop your skills, and will be very much looking for potential and motivation. Items to include are:

- drawings made from observation and imagination, using a variety of media
- life drawings
- project work in your specialised area of study made on your current course
- personal work in your specialisation made for yourself
- sketchbooks
- colour work made in a variety of media
- photography
- contextual studies or written work
- photographs of three-dimensional work as required, if it is not possible to transport it.

With respect to your specialist project work use the following examples as a starting point for ideas on what to include. As a rule, your portfolio should contain a sustained project made within your proposed area of study. Contact the course admissions tutor if you are unsure what to put in.

Fashion – drawings; sketches; fashion designs; photographs or actual examples of garments you have made; a collection of information on particular designers, fashion manufacturers or shops; a design project worked on to a brief.

Film, TV and Animation – a short film (on video or CD) that you may have made as part of a course project; scripts; storyboards; a subject-dedicated sketchbook; evidence that you regularly watch films and read reviews.

Fine Art – paintings and/or sculptures, photographs, textiles, and pieces of coursework, produced to a negotiated brief; original pieces, produced entirely from your own ideas; evidence that you read art magazines and visit exhibitions.

Graphic Design – lettering; samples of freehand drawing; examples of work showing page layout; projects related to advertising, publicity or packaging; typography; coursework completed to a brief such as a complete publicity campaign for a product; digitally manipulated images; evidence that you read design magazines and visit exhibitions.

Illustration – work done from direct observation; work related to a design and technology project (if applying for technical or scientific illustration courses); work done to a 'brief' – for example, a piece done to illustrate pages of a particular book, with sample text and notes explaining how you set out to emphasise particular aspects; evidence that you read appropriate literature and visit exhibitions.

Product Design – drawings, diagrams, computer-aided designs; working notes, showing that you understand the workshop processes necessary to manufacture the product; preliminary sketches; photographs of the finished article; evidence that you read design magazines and visit exhibitions.

SOME ADMISSIONS TUTORS' PREFERENCES

Tim Dunbar, recently an admissions tutor for the BA (Hons) course in Fine Art at Manchester Metropolitan University (now an administrator in the Art and Design Faculty)

'We send applicants a list suggesting the type of work to include, as follows:

- a range of work which demonstrates a high level of ability in your selected specialist area
- a selection of work which reveals a personal direction or area of concern
- evidence of drawing used as an investigative process and as a means of generating ideas
- sketchbooks/notebooks
- History of art/contextual studies files and evidence of written work (essays, critical reviews, etc).

'When we examine the portfolios we look for a sense of the individual student and evidence through their work of their take on the world – their own standpoint. If the portfolio contains life drawings, we want to see some kind of personality as opposed to domination by the life-class tutors. Projects should demonstrate their own interpretation of the brief through progressive stages.'

Sarah Horton, Course Leader, BA (Hons), Norwich School of Art and Design

'*Drawing:* evidence of life drawing can be useful because it demonstrates such a particular discipline, but any drawing that shows you can observe and interpret the world around you is important. Drawings can be any scale and in any medium, but a diversity of approaches shows exploration and a keenness to experiment.

'*Problem-solving:* your ability to solve visual problems can be demonstrated through design sheets or sketchbooks, but should show in detail how you would deal with design briefs or your own (if more Fine Art-based) issues or ideas. If anything, these are the most revealing parts of the interview, and for many staff it is more important than seeing finished pieces.

'*Diversity:* a diversity of work and a willingness to experiment are crucial. A good problem-solver needs to use any number of techniques and approaches, so you must show flexibility and adaptability. If you come with only one method of working, your methods will look narrow and limited.

'*Consistency:* as well as diversity you need to show that you can also take an idea and "run with it"; that you have developed, in some depth, one or more particular projects or themes.

'*Independence:* at degree level you will need to be able to generate work that is self-directed and independent. Your portfolio, therefore, needs to show that you have developed your own ways of working that haven't been directed solely by your tutors.

'*Critical/contextual studies:* most degree courses have a theoretical element, usually involving written work, so something that shows your ability to write is also important. Interviewers will also need to know that you are interested in the broader context of art and design. Even at its simplest level, you will be asked about practitioners who have influenced or impressed you and exhibitions you've recently visited.

'Finally, it is impossible to quantify the amount and type of work to take to an interview. While you should include a full range of work that isn't over-edited, you should select carefully rather than include absolutely everything you've ever made! Emphasise your most recent work as this is the work that best represents your current concerns. Because it is fresh in your mind this is also the work you'll be able to talk about with the most enthusiasm.

'The key to your portfolio is its organisation. Have a strong beginning and end, and order your work coherently in projects or subjects, giving most emphasis to recent work. Listen to advice from tutors: they have great expertise in helping students gain university places.

'For three-dimensional or large-scale work, bring good-quality photographs or slides. Better still, bring originals, but good reproductions will often suffice.'

David Bramston, Course Leader of the BA (Hons) Product Design course at the University of Lincoln

'I find that the National Diploma students have the best portfolios, but they have been focused for some time. But other students are not disadvantaged. We can spot talent and creativity from all sorts of work. What to put in a portfolio? We are not prescriptive, although we do want to see work students have done in their own time, not merely work required by the curriculum. If I see a portfolio containing nothing but coursework I am disappointed. Design is visual, so we like to see sketches and notebooks. Ten pieces would be about right – including pen and pencil sketches, collage and photographs, plus notes. (We do find that some students put in far too much text, however.) BUT if they cannot find ten really good pieces it is better to settle for seven, rather than include seven good ones and three dodgy ones! Interviewers tend to judge a portfolio by the worst piece in it. If students have padded with a less good piece – we might think "Is this really what they think is good enough?" It is not essential to bring in actual examples of 3D work. A student once brought a car full of sculptures. Photographs of the pieces would have been adequate.

'Knowing how to present the portfolio is important. It sounds elementary but candidates need to know how to open it! If they open it the wrong way round or pages become unclipped and fall out, the student will become flustered. Work need not be presented in chronological order but there must be a reason for the order. The first page is crucial. It could well remain open for five minutes while the interviewer asks questions – so if chronological order does not present work to its best advantage, another method is better.

'There must be some explanation of the work in the portfolio. This is best in the form of the brief the student was given or the idea they developed on their own inserted in clear plastic sheets between the pieces of work. I need a clear definition. For instance, if the project was to produce something using only a brown plastic chair that cost under £5.00 I need to know that. This type of explanation is even more important at institutions where the student is not there in person to talk through the portfolio.

'The entire portfolio should look professional – up to the standard expected of a designer, properly mounted with no fingerprints or lopsided mounting.'

Sandy Farrell, Programme Leader, HNC/D Fine Art, West Kent College (a partner college of the University of Greenwich)

'To be successful, students have to feel a compulsion to study art. They must need to do it. They should feel compelled to find ways of exploring and expressing themselves through visual art. They should demonstrate an awareness of the big stage that is the world of art and should have an idea of which part of it they want to occupy. I'm looking for physical evidence of all of this in the portfolio.'

Stephen Brigdale, Senior Lecturer in Photography, Southampton Solent University

'The portfolio and interview are key. We are interested in seeing samples of applicants' work and also in discovering how they articulate their practice – even though they are still at a formative stage.

'A mature applicant might only have photographic work to bring, but we expect to see a range of work from applicants drawn from A levels or Foundation courses – a selection of pieces from their chosen specialism but also supporting work from other areas – for example, drawings and design work. The work should be carefully edited and chosen to show a position of some kind. From this we can see the beginnings of an individual voice starting to emerge.

'We require an essay to be included in the portfolio too, since it is important for us to know that students will be capable of the written work that is demanded at degree level. The subject might be on some contextual aspect, showing that they understand the historical, social and cultural contexts of art and photography. Students with a media studies background might include as supplementary to their photography work a video, as well as an essay on a contemporary area of media practice. All the work in the portfolio should be professionally edited and presented.'

Debbie Cook, Tutor, Communication Art and Design, Royal College of Art and Postgraduate Coordinator, International Office, Central Saint Martins, University of the Arts London

'Ideally, we would like to see a portfolio that demonstrates a high level of visual skill, creativity, commitment and self-motivation. We would be looking for evidence of intellectual enquiry and cultural awareness.

'We would expect you to have completed a Foundation course and the resulting portfolio may include sketchbooks, ideas books, set projects, self-initiated work, finished pieces, work in progress, photographs, or three-dimensional work.

'We value a portfolio of work that includes continuity of ideas, and a series of related images that relate to each other in some way. We are interested in your research, thinking, and projects that show the development and progression of an idea. We particularly value self-initiated work because it tells us so much about you!

'Your portfolio should be self-explanatory – it may be viewed initially in your absence! Edit your work and play with the sequencing of images and projects until they unfold in such a way that they tell us who you are, and what you think.

'And above all we are looking for potential.'

Annette Bellwood, International Academic Coordinator, London College of Communication, University of the Arts London

'A portfolio should speak for itself and tell us about you ideas, your passions and your personal approach to working. A commitment to the subject and an engagement with projects should be evident.

'You need to be self-motivated and have the capacity to work independently and this should be reflected in your portfolio. We are interested in the journey your work takes, your ability to recognise and generate ideas, explore their possibilities and develop them. This process of thinking and working, within a broad cultural context, is crucial.

'Finally, present your work in a clear and organised way to ensure that it communicates all that you want it to.'

The prospectus for the University College for the Creative Arts states:

'Work within your portfolio should reflect your individual identity and should show creative thinking and investigation. You should include work that reveals your capacity to develop a project through all stages from start to finish. In addition, your portfolio should demonstrate the ability to explore different approaches and solutions to art and design challenges. You can include sketchbooks, notebooks and contact sheets as well as finished work.'

CHECKLIST

☐ **Round up your work**
☐ **Check out portfolio specification**
☐ **Purchase portfolio**
☐ **Attend evening classes**
☐ **Review portfolio**
☐ **Set targets and deadlines**
☐ **Photograph 3D work**
☐ **Label portfolio**
☐ **Adapt portfolio to particular specification.**

9

THE INTERVIEW

This chapter is about how to make the most of your interview. Although the format of the interview will vary from college to college and there are differences between interviewing for a Foundation course and a specialist degree course, the following guidelines will be of help to you. Make sure that you read this chapter in conjunction with the chapter 'Putting together your portfolio'.

WHAT IS THE PURPOSE OF THE INTERVIEW?

Interviews are there to help art schools find the most appropriate students and to help students find the most appropriate art schools. Most people who fear interviews do so either because they misunderstand their purpose or because they do not know what to expect and imagine the worst. We worry that we will be asked impossible questions, that the interviewers will not like us or that they will try to catch us out; we worry that we will not be good enough.

Consider this: Art schools exist because students want to study Art and Design. Without the students there would be no colleges, no lecturers, no admissions tutors and no courses. In other words, where would art schools be without you? You are the single most important element in the educational process and, as such, it is not in any college's interest to try and make life difficult for you. Yes, interviewers will be trying to find out if you are suited to the course for which you are applying and, yes, they will be carefully considering both you and your work and, yes, you can expect to be asked some challenging questions, but try to take a positive attitude. Most people are nervous at interview; admissions tutors understand this and will make allowances. They are there to try to get the best from you.

Also remember that the interview provides you with an opportunity to assess a prospective college. Hopefully, you will have visited the college before your interview and checked things out, but a second look around will not do you any harm. Although you may have already met some of the lecturers, since you will probably be studying with some of the people who will be interviewing you, check them out too. For an example of students at interview please see photo 8 in the colour section (between pp. 56 and 57).

WHAT TO EXPECT

In some colleges you will deliver your portfolio for consideration prior to being offered an interview. At others, the admissions tutors will initially look at your work without you and then ask you in to discuss it with them. This can happen ten minutes after they take it or sometimes later that day. In many instances, especially at interviews for degree courses, you will begin your interview by being asked to present your work briefly to an interviewer or panel of interviewers who will be seeing it for the first time. In many cases, a conversation will begin as you show your work, developing into a more formal question-and-answer session towards the end of the interview. However, interviews vary from college to college, so before attending read through the college's literature to find out what the format will be.

Interviews vary in length from as little as five or ten minutes, to up to 30 or 40 minutes for specialist degree courses. Don't be surprised or worried if the interview feels as if it was very short. Time seems to pass much more rapidly in this kind of situation. Also remember that the interviewers are experts, know what they are looking for and often will be able to come to a decision quickly. This is particularly the case for Foundation courses where admissions tutors will frequently have to see literally hundreds of students in a matter of weeks.

In some cases you will find out if you have been successful on the day, but in most you will be notified by post in due course.

PREPARING

It is impossible to know exactly what you will be asked at interview, and in some ways it is not helpful to be overly prepared since it is much better to allow a discussion to develop naturally, answering the questions that you have been asked rather than insisting that you talk about what you have been reading up on. As a guide consider the following:

1 | Why have you applied for this particular course?
2 | Why have you applied to study it here?
3 | Which artists have influenced you?
4 | What are you hoping to do in the future?

If you have been conscientious about choosing a course, you will be able to make a positive response to the first two questions. (Make sure that you have read the relevant sections in the chapters on Foundation and degree courses, pages 5–15 and 17–30.) Rereading your notes, looking through the course prospectus and talking things through with others will all help. Rather than trying to 'revise' for the answers that you think they will want, simply remind yourself of what you have done, so that you can respond honestly.

With respect to question 3, before going to the interview look through your work. Consider the connections between your work and that of others. If you have worked on a written project, reread it. Looking through your sketchbooks can also help, since they are, in part, a record of your creative process. You will probably have collected cuttings and postcards. These visual prompts will help to remind you of your influences.

During the period leading up to your interview, make a point of getting out and about. Make sure that you visit some exhibitions. In addition to looking at well-known exhibits in museums, go and see a show of new work. Also keep up to date by reading the arts pages of national newspapers and periodicals (there is a reading list in the 'Further information' chapter).

If you are applying for a place on a Foundation course it is likely that your future plans will include taking a degree. You can say this. If you are applying for a place on a specialist degree course, jotting down a few notes to help you think things through may be helpful in preparing for the fourth question. Whatever your thoughts might be, don't worry if you cannot come up with a complete answer. That is perfectly normal. It would be a pretty boring world to live in if we all knew exactly what we were going to do in the future!

Assuming that you have done your homework and know as much as possible about the course, you will not need to use up valuable time asking questions about course structure or discussing specific issues such as funding. If you are given the chance to ask questions or make comments, it is normally much better to respond to what is currently being discussed than to set your own agenda. Perhaps the best way to prepare for this is by taking a mock interview, which will give you a feel for how an interview develops.

Many schools and colleges offer mock interviews to their own students and in some cases to external candidates. If you have the chance to do one, make sure you don't miss out. Mock interviews provide excellent preparation.

As well as thinking about the kind of questions that you might be asked, it is also important to consider a few practicalities. For example, how will you be travelling to the interview? If you are applying to a local art school you may only have to make a short journey. You may be applying to a course a long way from home, so consider the logistics. In some cases an overnight stay may be necessary. Also think about how you intend to transport your work. In many instances you will be able to carry everything in a portfolio. Most colleges are happy to look at photographs of three-dimensional or larger pieces. However, in some situations it will be necessary to take this work with you. You may need to ask a friend for help or to ask the college for advice.

Practise your presentation technique. Can you comfortably manage your portfolio or is it too heavy? Once again mock interviews are an excellent way to identify and resolve any potential problems.

Discussing your work with art college or university teachers can be a daunting experience and you will need to practise before your interview. As a general rule of thumb, try to structure any discussion of your work as follows:

1 | Where the idea for the piece came from. This is an opportunity to talk about artists whose work you like, exhibitions you have visited, or previous work that you have produced.
2 | How your ideas were realised in the piece. You could talk about the composition, the materials and the techniques you used as well as what the work represents.
3 | Where the work will lead you. You could talk about what you will work on next, what you might have done differently, or how the piece has led you to investigate other artists or techniques.

The interviewer will help you by asking you questions and possibly suggesting other areas of research.

THE NIGHT BEFORE
Assuming that you are well organised, there should be nothing left to do except relax and get a good night's sleep, so make sure that you do! Easy to say, difficult to do. We all get nervous before a big day and you might find it difficult to

switch off. Don't worry if this happens – it just means that you're normal. Try doing something to take your mind off things, like watching a film, chatting with friends or maybe taking a little gentle exercise. Try not to worry. Be positive. Remember art schools cannot exist without students!

THE INTERVIEW ITSELF: SOME HELPFUL TIPS

Make sure you arrive early. You don't want to be rushing around at the last minute.

Dress comfortably. Your interviewers will be far more interested in who you are and what you do than what you wear. If your hair is bright blue and shaved on one side, fine. If it isn't, well that's fine too. You will need much more than a good hairstyle to get into art school!

Make eye contact. If you are asked to show your work, make sure that you do not turn your back on the interviewers. Try to position your portfolio between yourself and the people you are speaking to or, if you are standing side by side, turn towards them from time to time.

Be willing to listen as well as talk. Sometimes when we are nervous we talk too much. Try to listen carefully to the questions that you are being asked. You will respond far more intelligently if you understand what has been said. If you do not understand, don't be afraid to ask for further explanation. Sometimes there will be pauses in the conversation. Don't let this unnerve you: the tutors are just concentrating while they look at your work.

Be willing to consider new ideas. You will be very difficult to teach if you find it hard to keep an open mind. Try not to become defensive if some of your responses to questions are challenged.

Be yourself. You don't need to put on an act. Above all never try to bluff or lie. You will always be found out, so only show your own work and if you do not know something then say so.

Above all, be enthusiastic. Don't be afraid to express your commitment and passion for your subject. You will have worked very hard up to this point. Let your interviewers know that this matters to you. Try not to be cool. Art schools are looking for motivated students.

HOPE

Use the acronym HOPE as a reminder of the personal qualities that you will try to display at interview:

- Honest
- Open-minded
- Prepared
- Enthusiastic!

AFTERWARDS   Meet up with a friend and talk things through: this will help you to put things into perspective. Also it will greatly help your fellow students if you give them some feedback. They may not have had an interview yet and your experience will be beneficial. A day or two later, when you have had the chance to reflect a little, make a note of anything that sticks in your mind that might be helpful for next time.

SOME ADMISSIONS TUTORS' ADVICE

FOUNDATION STUDIES

Bill Watson, International Coordinator, Camberwell College of Arts (a college of the University of the Arts London)

'In interview, the reviewers are looking for students who demonstrate curiosity about why the world looks like it does. One expects the beginning of an interest in and knowledge of art and design; the context of art and design. Who does art and design and why? What magazines, books, TV programmes, is a student interested in and why? Have they ever visited a museum, gallery, film or concert on their own without the prompting of school, college or friends? Can they name a living designer or architect? What has been the most striking visual experience they have had in the last year? Answers to these questions reveal whether a student's education has led them passively to this point or whether they have a genuine desire for discovery.'

Roy Naylor, Head of Foundation Studies, Winchester School of Art, University of Southampton

'Students are normally interviewed by me or another experienced member of the department staff. We spend between 20 and 30 minutes with each applicant. During this time we expect them to talk through their portfolio, which we will normally have looked at in advance and will ask questions about.

'Interview questions focus on both how and why the work was produced and how it might develop, and on wider issues – for example, on the applicant's interest in the work of other designers or artists. I will expect them to be able to talk about books, journals and shows, and to be able to get under the skin of a subject. I want to know what they have read that is related to art and design – like *Art Monthly*, *Creative Review*, *Design Week* or *Frieze*. Can they talk about favourite artists and designers? Have they done any research in their own time? Visited galleries and exhibitions? It is not always possible for students who live miles from a large town or city to make many live visits but anyone can use the internet and do some research there. They could also ask if they could have reading rights at their local art school library. Many will say yes, even though they probably will not allow them to borrow books. All these activities show evidence of initiative – which course tutors like very much!'

Degree and Higher National Diploma courses

Sarah Horton, Course Leader, BA (Hons) Fine Art, Norwich School of Art and Design

'Above all else, you will need to show a seriousness and enthusiasm for your work. Make sure you convince your interviewers that you are passionate about your subject and the particular course you are being interviewed for, as no course leader is interested in a student who lacks energy, enthusiasm and motivation. Also, make sure you know exactly why you are applying for that particular course. Ideally, you will have already visited it, so talk about that experience.

'Secondly, more than anything else at interview, we are trying to measure potential – your potential to work hard and capacity to improve. None of this is achievable if you are not open-minded. We are interested in students who have a thirst for new ideas and are willing to learn. If you are closed to new ideas it will be impossible to teach you, and your place will be offered to someone else!'

**Bryan Preston,
Subject Leader,
BA/HND
Photomedia
Production,
Plymouth
College of Art
and Design**

'All applicants have a 30-minute interview with two members of staff. We try to make the interview situation as relaxed as possible. We want the applicants to give their best, because we want the best students! Staff take the interview procedure very seriously: successful choice of students ensures a successful future for the programme.

'I always remind staff to try to interview against the background of opportunity the individual applicant has experienced. We have different criteria for accepting students from, for example, Foundation or BTEC National Diploma courses.

'With applicants who bring 2D portfolios, we usually view the portfolio without the student being present before the actual interview. This allows us to interview the applicant – not the portfolio! Those with show reels should always remember that if the interview is 20 minutes we do not want to see a 50-minute sequence, no matter how good! We are of course interested in the work, but our main interest is in the individual. What is their potential for the next two or three years? How do they relate to other people? How well do they work in a group situation? What broader interests do they have in media and other aspects of life?

'Finally, we like to know that the students have visited us for an open day and are therefore informed about the programme they are applying for. It's as much a case of an applicant accepting us as it is us accepting them!'

Sandy Farrell, Programme Leader, HNC/D Fine Art, West Kent College (a partner college of the University of Greenwich)

'I don't hold formal interviews. I believe in getting to know the student before looking at their work. (I am able to do this because it's quite a small course.) So I take them for a walk around the campus, show them the facilities, talk to them – then by the time I come to look at the portfolio they are relaxed and less nervous. I find a quiet corner somewhere in the college to do this, rather than sit behind a desk in my office. I ask them to talk me through the work and explain what it means to them. I also ask a few questions. For instance, I asked one student last week if she thought that she had the determination to carry something through once she had decided on it. Her reply was that she got up every day to do yoga between 4am and 6am because this was important to her.'

Stephen Brigdale, Senior Lecturer in Photography, Southampton Solent University

'The selection process varies from place to place. Some colleges hold panel interviews or interviews with two members of staff. Here we use one-to-one interviews held during the course of a whole day during which students are given tours and also contact with current students.

'I would advise students at interview to be themselves. Their own opinions are of interest and importance. They must be prepared to talk – for instance about contemporary art and design work that they have seen in current exhibitions and their viewpoint on it. And they should not be afraid to ask questions.'

Tim Dunbar, recently an admissions tutor for the BA (Hons) course in Fine Art at Manchester Metropolitan University (now an administrator in the Art and Design Faculty)

'Interviews last between 20 and 30 minutes and are informal discussions, centred on the applicants' work, areas of special interest and reasons for wishing to study Fine Art in Manchester.

'Art is a passion. Students need to be 100% committed. This is not like doing a degree in pharmacy which leads to a particular job. There is no specific career route for artists. They will have to find their own way. Unless the enthusiasm is there they will not make it. Natural talent with no sense of industry will not do!

'Evidence of this enthusiasm should come out during the interview. We expect candidates to know the work of current artists like Damien Hirst and Rachel Whiteread, to have heard of the Saatchi Gallery, to have read widely, if possible to have visited galleries and exhibitions. They should be able to talk with enthusiasm about all of these – as they should do when displaying their own work to us.'

David Bramston, Course Leader for the BA (Hons) Product Design course at the University of Lincoln

'Students often worry about the correct dress for an interview. My personal view is that they should make an effort – but go for smart casual. An Armani suit and tie would be over the top. Trainers and denim would be equally unsuitable. Black jeans, chinos, open-neck shirt, an informal skirt and top will be fine. Once here, of course, they will live in T-shirt and jeans.

'We believe in one-to-one interviews. By far the most important aspect of the selection process is the student's portfolio. Unlike some institutions we do not pre-examine them. Instead, the student is asked during the interview to spend ten minutes presenting the portfolio to the interviewer. They can also expect questions aiming to find out whether they know what product design is. Have they read around the subject? Do they watch design programmes or read journals such as *New Design* or *Icon*? They might also be asked about their own ambitions. Where do they expect to be in ten years' time?'

CHECKLIST

- ☐ Visit exhibitions
- ☐ Read arts pages of national newspapers and magazines
- ☐ Review portfolio
- ☐ Conduct a mock interview
- ☐ Check interview date, time and location
- ☐ Find out how to get to interview.

FURTHER INFORMATION

These books can be ordered from Trotman Publishing Ltd,
Tel: 0870 900 2665, Website: www.careers-portal.co.uk

APPLICATIONS (FOUNDATION AND DEGREE COURSES)

Trotman's Green Guides: Art, Design and Performing Arts Courses, published by Trotman

DEGREE COURSE APPLICATIONS

UCAS, Rosehill, New Barn Lane, Cheltenham, Gloucestershire GL52 3LA, Tel: 01242 227788, **www.ucas.com**

Oxford Colleges Admissions Office, University Offices, Wellington Square, Oxford OX1 2JD, Tel: 01865 270207, **www.ox.ac.uk**

How to Complete your UCAS Application, published by Trotman

Degree Course Offers, by Brian Heap, published by Trotman

University and College Entrance – The Official Guide (also known as 'the Big Book'), published by UCAS

FUNDING

Students' Money Matters, by Gwenda Thomas, published by Trotman

UCAS financial information, **www.ucas.com/studentfinance**

Student Loans Company, Tel: 0800 405010, **www.slc.co.uk**

Local Authority student support information, **www.dfes.gov.uk/studentsupport**

CAREERS

A good starting point is Trotman's careers website **www.careers-portal.co.uk**

Art and Design Uncovered, by Emma Caprez, published by Trotman

Careers in Art and Design, by Noel Chapman, published by Kogan Page

Q&A Studying Art and Design, published by Trotman

CRAC Degree Courses Guides: Art and Design Studies with History of Art and Design, published by Trotman

Becoming a Product Designer: A Guide to Careers in Design, published by John Wiley

ART AND DESIGN MAGAZINES

This list only scrapes the surface of the publications available. The best places to look for art and design magazines are museum and gallery bookshops, which carry wide selections.

AG (photography)
Architectural Journal
Architectural Review
Art Monthly
Art Review
B&W (photography)
Blueprint (design)
British Journal of Photography
Ceramic Review
Ceramics Monthly
Creative Review
Modern Painters
Photography Monthly
PLUK (photography listings)
Portfolio (photography)
Tate Magazine

WEB MAGAZINES

A List Apart (web design): **www.alistapart.com**
Artistica (graphic design): **www.artistica.org**
Art Magazine: **www.artmagazine.co.uk**
ARTnews: **www.artnewsonline.com**
Graphic Arts Monthly: **www.gammag.com**
Juxtapoz Art & Culture Magazine: **www.juxtapoz.com**
NY Arts: **www.nyartsmagazine.com**

ART AND DESIGN BODIES

Applied Arts Scotland
6 Darnaway Street
Edinburgh EH3 6BG
Tel: 0131 220 5070
ApArtScot@aol.com

The Arts Council of
England
14 Great Peter Street
London SW1P 3NQ
www.artscouncil.org.uk

Arts Council of Northern
Ireland
MacNeice House
77 Malone Road
Belfast BT9 6AQ
www.artscouncil-ni.org

Arts Council of Wales
Holst House
9 Museum Place
Cardiff CF10 3NX
www.artswales.org.uk

Association of
Photographers
9–10 Domingo Street
London EC1Y 0TA
www.the-aop.org

British Film Institute
21 Stephen Street
London W1T 1LN
www.bfi.org.uk

Crafts Council
44a Pentonville Road
London N1 9BY
www.craftscouncil.org.uk

The Design Council
34 Bow Street
London WC2E 7DL
www.design-council.org.uk

INTERNATIONAL STUDENTS

British Council
www.britishcouncil.org

English UK
www.englishuk.com

UKCOSA
www.ukcosa.org.uk

INSTITUTION
ADDRESSES

UCAS

**University of Wales,
Aberystwyth**
Old College
King Street
Aberystwyth
Ceredigion
SY23 2AX
Tel: 01970 623111
Fax: 01970 627410
ug-admissions@aber.ac.uk
www.aber.ac.uk

**Amersham and Wycombe
College**
Stanley Hill Centre
Amersham
Buckinghamshire
HP7 9HN
Tel: 01494 735555
Fax: 01494 735566
info@amersham.ac.uk
www.amersham.ac.uk

Anglia Ruskin University
Cambridge Campus
East Road
Cambridge
CB1 1PT
Tel: 01223 363271
Fax: 01223 352973
answers@apu.ac.uk
www.apu.ac.uk

Arts Institute at Bournemouth
Wallisdown
Poole
BH12 5HH
Tel: 01202 533011
Fax: 01202 537729
general@aib.ac.uk
www.aib.ac.uk

Barking College
Dagenham Road
Romford
Essex
RM7 0XU
Tel: 01708 770000
Fax: 01708 770007
admissions@barking-coll.ac.uk
www.barkingcollege.ac.uk

Barnfield College, Luton
New Bedford Road
Luton
LU2 7BF
Tel: 01582 569700
Fax: 01582 492928
www.barnfield.ac.uk

Barnsley College
PO Box No 266
Church Street
Barnsley
S70 2YW
Tel: 01226 216171/216172
Fax: 01226 216166
programme.enquiries@barnsley.ac.uk
www.barnsley.ac.uk

**Basingstoke College of
Technology**
Worting Road
Basingstoke
Hampshire
RG21 8TN
Tel: 01256 354141
Fax: 01256 306444
info@bcot.ac.uk
www.bcot.ac.uk

Bath Spa University
Newton Park
Newton St Loe
Bath
BA2 9BN
Tel: 01225 875875
Fax: 01225 875444
enquiries@bathspa.ac.uk
www.bathspa.ac.uk

Bedford College
Cauldwell Street
Bedford
MK42 9AH
Tel: 01234 291000
Fax: 01234 342674
www.bedford.ac.uk

University of Birmingham
Edgbaston
Birmingham
B15 2TT
Tel: 0121 414 344
Fax: 0121 44 3971
admissions@bham.ac.uk
www.bham.ac.uk

Birmingham City College
The Council House
Soho Road
Handsworth
Birmingham
B21 9DP
Tel: 0121 741 1000
Fax: 0121 523 4447
enquiries@citycol.ac.uk
www.citycol.ac.uk

Bishop Burton College
Bishop Burton
Beverley
East Riding of Yorkshire
HU17 8QG
Tel: 01964 553000
Fax: 01964 553101
enquiries@bishopb-college.ac.uk
www.bishopb-college.ac.uk

Bishop Grosseteste College
Lincoln
Lincolnshire
LN1 3DY
Tel: 01522 527347
Fax: 01522 530243
registry@bgc.ac.uk
www.bgc.ac.uk

Blackburn College
Feilden Street
Blackburn
BB2 1LH
Tel: 01254 55144
Fax: 01254 263947
studentservices@blackburn.ac.uk
www.blackburn.ac.uk

**Blackpool and the Fylde
College**
Ashfield Road
Bispham
Blackpool
FY2 0HB
Tel: 01253 352352
Fax: 01253 356127
visitors@blackpool.ac.uk
www.blackpool.ac.uk

University of Bolton
Deane Road
Bolton
Lancashire
BL3 5AB
Tel: 01204 900600

Fax: 01204 399074
enquiries@bolton.ac.uk
www.bolton.ac.uk

Bournemouth University
Poole House
Talbot Campus
Fern Barrow
Bournemouth
BH12 5BB
Tel: 01202 524111
Fax: 01202 702736
prospectus@bournemouth.ac.uk
www.bournemouth.ac.uk

University of Bradford
Richmond Road
Bradford
BD7 1DP
Tel: 01274 232323
Fax: 01274 236260
course-enquiries@bradford.ac.uk
www.brad.ac.uk

Bradford College
Great Horton Road
Bradford
BD7 1AY
Tel: 01274 753004
Fax: 01274 753173
admissions@bilk.ac.uk
www.bilk.ac.uk

University of Brighton
Mithras House
Lewes Road
Brighton
BN2 4AT
Tel: 01273 600900
Fax: 01273 642825
admissions@brighton.ac.uk
www.brighton.ac.uk

Bristol UWE
Frenchay Campus
Coldharbour Lane
Bristol
BS16 1QY
Tel: 0117 965 6261
Fax: 0117 344 2810
admissions@uwe.ac.uk
www.uwe.ac.uk

City of Bristol College
College Green Centre
St George's Road

Bristol
BS1 5UA
Tel: 0117 904 5000
Fax: 0117 904 5050
enquiries@cityofbristol.ac.uk
www.cityofbristol.ac.uk

Buckinghamshire Chilterns University College
Queen Alexandra Road
High Wycombe
Buckinghamshire
HP11 2JZ
Tel: 01494 522141
Fax: 01494 524392
admissions@bcuc.ac.uk
www.bcuc.ac.uk

Camberwell College of Arts
University of the Arts London
Peckham Road
London
SE5 8UF
Tel: 020 7514 6302
Fax: 020 7514 6310
enquiries@camb.arts.ac.uk
www.camb.arts.ac.uk

Canterbury Christ Church University
North Holmes Road
Canterbury
Kent
CT1 1QU
Tel: 01227 767700
Fax: 01227 470442
admissions@cant.ac.uk
www.cant.ac.uk

University of Wales Institute, Cardiff
Student Recruitment and Admissions
Western Avenue
Cardiff
CF5 2SG
Tel: 029 2041 6070
Fax: 029 2041 6286
uwicinfo@uwic.ac.uk
www.uwic.ac.uk

Carshalton College
Nightingale Road
Sutton

SM5 2EJ
Tel: 020 8770 6800
Fax: 020 8770 6899
www.carshalton.ac.uk

UCE Birmingham
Perry Barr
Birmingham
B42 2SU
Tel: 0121 331 5000
Fax: 0121 356 2875
prospectus@uce.ac.uk
www.uce.ac.uk

University of Central Lancashire
Preston
Lancashire
PR1 2HE
Tel: 01772 201201
Fax: 01772 892946
c.enquiries@uclan.ac.uk
www.uclan.ac.uk

Central School of Speech and Drama
Embassy Theatre
Eton Avenue
London
NW3 3HY
Tel: 020 7722 8183
Fax: 020 7722 4132
www.cssd.ac.uk

Central Saint Martins College of Art and Design
University of the Arts London
Southampton Row
London
WC1B 4AP
Tel: 020 7514 7000
Fax: 020 7514 7024
applications@csm.arts.ac.uk
www.csm.arts.ac.uk

Chelsea College of Art and Design
University of the Arts London
Manresa Road
London
SW3 6LS
Tel: 020 7514 7750
Fax: 020 7514 7778

enquiries@chelsea.arts.ac.uk
www.chelsea.arts.ac.uk

University of Chester
Parkgate Road
Chester
Cheshire
CH1 4BJ
Tel: 01244 375444
Fax: 01244 392820
enquiries@chester.ac.uk
www.chester.ac.uk

Chesterfield College
Infirmary Road
Chesterfield
Derbyshire
S41 7NG
Tel: 01246 500500
Fax: 01246 500587
www.chesterfield.ac.uk

University of Chichester
Bishop Otter Campus
College Lane
Chichester
West Sussex
PO19 6PE
Tel: 01243 816000
Fax: 01243 816080
admissions@ucc.ac.uk
www.ucc.ac.uk

City and Islington College
The Marlborough Building
383 Holloway Road
Islington
London
N7 0RN
Tel: 020 7700 9200
Fax: 020 7700 9222
www.candi.ac.uk

Cleveland College of Art and Design
Administration Centre
Green Lane
Linthorpe
Middlesbrough
TS5 7RJ
Tel: 01642 288000
Fax: 01642 288828
admissions@ccad.ac.uk
www.ccad.ac.uk

Colchester Institute
Sheepen Road
Colchester
CO3 3LL
Tel: 01206 518000
Fax: 01206 763041
info@colch-inst.ac.uk
www.colch-inst.ac.uk

Coleg Sir Gâr
Graig Campus
Sandy Road
Llanelli
SA15 4DN
Tel: 01554 748000
Fax: 01554 756088
admissions@colegsirgar.ac.uk
www.colegsirgar.ac.uk

College of St Mark & St John
Derriford Road
Plymouth
PL6 8BH
Tel: 01752 636890
Fax: 01752 636819
admissions@marjon.ac.uk
www.marjon.ac.uk

Cornwall College
Head Office
Lombard House
8 Palace Road
St Austell
Cornwall
PL25 4BU
Tel: 01726 222718
Fax: 01726 65926
ccho@st-austell.ac.uk
www.cornwall.ac.uk

Coventry University
Priory Street
Coventry
CV1 5FB
Tel: 024 7688 7688
Fax: 024 7688 8638
Info.reg@coventry.ac.uk
www.coventry.ac.uk

University College for the Creative Arts at Canterbury, Epsom, Farnham, Maidstone and Rochester
Falkner Road
Farnham
Surrey
GU9 7DS
Tel: 01252 722441
info@ucreative.ac.uk
www.ucreative.ac.uk

Croydon College
Fairfield
Croydon
CR9 1DX
Tel: 020 8686 5700
Fax: 020 8760 5880
info@croydon.ac.uk
www.croydon.ac.uk

Cumbria Institute of the Arts
Brampton Road
Carlisle
Cumbria
CA3 9AY
Tel: 01228 400300
Fax: 01228 514491
info@cumbria.ac.uk
www.cumbria.ac.uk

Dartington College of Arts
Totnes
Devon
TQ9 6EJ
Tel: 01803 862224
Fax: 01803 863569
registry@dartington.ac.uk
www.dartington.ac.uk

De Montfort University
The Gateway
Leicester
LE1 9BH
Tel: 0116 255 1551
Fax: 0116 255 0307
enquiry@dmu.ac.uk
www.dmu.ac.uk

University of Derby
Kedleston Road
Derby
DE22 1GB
Tel: 01332 590500
Fax: 01332 294861
admissions@derby.ac.uk
www.derby.ac.uk

Dewsbury College
Halifax Road
Dewsbury
West Yorkshire
WF13 2AS
Tel: 01924 465916/436221
Fax: 01924 457047
info@dewsbury.ac.uk
www.dewsbury.ac.uk

Doncaster College
Waterdale
Doncaster
DN1 3EX
Tel: 01302 553553
Fax: 01302 553559
webmaster@don.ac.uk
www.don.ac.uk

Dudley College of Technology
The Broadway
Dudley
DY1 4AS
Tel: 01384 363000
Fax: 01384 363311
student.services@dudleycol.ac.uk
www.dudleycol.ac.uk

University of Dundee
Perth Road
Dundee
DD1 4HN
Tel: 01382 344000
Fax: 01382 345500
srs@dundee.ac.uk
www.dundee.ac.uk

University of East Anglia
The Registry
Norwich
Norfolk
NR4 7TJ
Tel: 01603 456161
Fax: 01603 458553
admissions@uea.ac.uk
www.uea.ac.uk

University of East London
Barking Campus
Longbridge Road
Dagenham
Essex
RM8 2AS
Tel: 020 8223 3000
Fax: 020 8507 7799
admiss@uel.ac.uk
www.uel.ac.uk

East Surrey College (Reigate School of Art and Design)
Claremont Road
Redhill
Surrey
RH1 2JX
Tel: 01737 772611
Fax: 01737 768641
www.esc.org.uk

University of Edinburgh
Secretary's Office
Old College
South Bridge
Edinburgh
EH8 9YL
Tel: 0131 650 1000
Fax: 0131 650 2147
Communications.office@ed.ac.uk
www.ed.ac.uk

Edinburgh College of Art
Lauriston Place
Edinburgh
EH3 9DF
Tel: 0131 221 6000
Fax: 0131 221 6001
registration@eca.ac.uk
www.eca.ac.uk

Exeter College
Victoria House
33–36 Queen Street
Exeter
Devon
EX4 8QD
Tel: 01392 205222
Fax: 01392 210282
admissions@exe-coll.ac.uk
www.exe-coll.ac.uk

University College Falmouth
Woodlane
Falmouth
Cornwall
TR11 4RA
Tel: 01326 211077
Fax: 01326 212261
admissions@falmouth.ac.uk
www.falmouth.ac.uk

University of Glamorgan
Llantwit Road
Treforest
Pontypridd
Rhondda Cynon Taff

CF37 1DL
Tel: 01443 480480
Fax: 01443 480558
enquiries@glam.ac.uk
www.glam.ac.uk

Glasgow School of Art
167 Renfrew Street
Glasgow
G3 6RQ
Tel: 0141 353 4500
Fax: 0141 353 4746
info@gsa.ac.uk
www.gsa.ac.uk

University of Gloucestershire
PO Box 220
The Park Campus
Cheltenham
Gloucestershire
GL50 2QF
Tel: 01242 532700
Fax: 01242 543334
admissions@glos.ac.uk
www.glos.ac.uk

Goldsmiths, University of London
Lewisham
London
SE14 6NW
Tel: 020 7919 7766
Fax: 020 7919 7509
admissions@gold.ac.uk
www.goldsmiths.ac.uk

University of Greenwich
Maritime Greenwich Campus
Park Row
Greenwich
SE10 9LS
Tel: 020 8331 8000 / 0800 005006
Fax: 020 8331 8145
courseinfo@gre.ac.uk
www.gre.ac.uk

Herefordshire College of Art and Design
Folly Lane
Hereford
HR1 1LT
Tel: 01432 273359
Fax: 01432 341099
hcad@hereford-art-col.ac.uk
www.hereford-art-col.ac.uk

University of Hertfordshire
College Lane
Hatfield
Hertfordshire
AL10 9AB
Tel: 01707 284000
Fax: 01707 284115
admissions@herts.ac.uk
www.herts.ac.uk

University of Huddersfield
Queensgate
Huddersfield
HD1 3DH
Tel: 01484 422288
Fax: 01484 516151
admissions@hud.ac.uk
www.hud.ac.uk

University of Hull
Admissions Office
Cottingham Road
Hull
HU6 7RX
Tel: 01482 466100
Fax: 01482 442290
admissions@hull.ac.uk
www.hull.ac.uk

Inverness College
UHI Millennium Institute
3 Longman Road
Inverness
IV1 1SA
Tel: 01463 273000
Fax: 01463 711977
admissions.officer@inverness.uhi.ac.uk
www.inverness.uhi.ac.uk

University of Kent
The Registry
Canterbury
Kent
CT2 7NZ
Tel: 01227 764000
Fax: 01227 827077
recruitment@kent.ac.uk
www.kent.ac.uk

Kingston University
Cooper House
40–46 Surbiton Road
Kingston-upon-Thames
KT1 2HX
Tel: 020 8547 2000
Fax: 020 8547 7857

Admissions-info@kingston.ac.uk
www.kingston.ac.uk

Lancaster University
Bailrigg
Lancaster
LA1 4YW
Tel: 01524 65201
Fax: 01524 846243
ugadmissions@lancaster.ac.uk
www.lancs.ac.uk

University of Leeds
Woodhouse Lane
Leeds
LS2 9JT
Tel: 0113 243 1751
Fax: 0113 244 3923
prospectus@leeds.ac.uk
www.leeds.ac.uk

Leeds College of Art and Design
Jacob Kramer Building
Blenheim Walk
Leeds
LS2 9AQ
Tel: 0113 202 8000
Fax: 0113 202 8001
info@leeds-art.ac.uk
www.leeds-art.ac.uk

Leeds Metropolitan University
Calverley Street
Leeds
LS1 3HE
Tel: 0113 283 2600
Fax: 0113 283 3114
Course-enquiries@lmu.ac.uk
www.lmu.ac.uk

Lews Castle College
UHI Millennium Institute
Stornoway
Western Isles
HS2 0XR
Tel: 01851 770000
Fax: 01851 770001
aofficele@lews.uhi.ac.uk
www.lews.uhi.ac.uk

University of Lincoln
Brayford Pool
Lincoln
LN6 7TS
Tel: 01522 882000

Fax: 01522 882088
marketing@lincoln.ac.uk
www.lincoln.ac.uk

Liverpool Hope University
Hope Park
Liverpool
L16 9JD
Tel: 0151 291 3000
Fax: 0151 291 3100
admission@hope.ac.uk
www.hope.ac.uk

Liverpool John Moores University
Roscoe Court
4 Rodney Street
Liverpool
L1 2TZ
Tel: 0151 231 2121
Fax: 0151 231 5632
recruitment@livjm.ac.uk
www.livjm.ac.uk

London Metropolitan University
Admissions Office
160–220 Holloway Road
London
N7 8DB
Tel: 020 7423 0000
Fax: 020 7753 3272
admissions@londonmet.ac.uk
www.londonmet.ac.uk

Loughborough University
Loughborough
Leicestershire
LE11 3TU
Tel: 01509 263171
Fax: 01509 223905
admissions@lboro.ac.uk
www.lboro.ac.uk

Lowestoft College
St Peter's Street
Lowestoft
NR32 2NB
Tel: 01502 583521
Fax: 01502 500031
info@lowestoft.ac.uk
www.lowestoft.ac.uk

University of Luton
Park Square
Luton

LU1 3JU
Tel: 01582 734111
Fax: 01582 743400
admissions@luton.ac.uk
www.luton.ac.uk

City College Manchester
141 Barlow Moor Road
Didsbury
Manchester
M20 2PQ
Tel: 0161 957 1790
Fax: 0161 446 1185
admissions@ccm.ac.uk
www.ccm.ac.uk

Manchester Metropolitan University
All Saints Building
All Saints
Manchester
M15 6BH
Tel: 0161 247 2000
Fax: 0161 247 6390
enquiries@mmu.ac.uk
www.mmu.ac.uk

Middlesex University
Admissions and Enquiries
White Hart Lane
Enfield
London
N17 8HR
Tel: 020 8411 5898
Fax: 020 8411 5649
admissions@mdx.ac.uk
www.mdx.ac.uk

Moray College
UHI Millennium Institute
Moray Street
Elgin
IV30 1JJ
Tel: 01343 576000
Fax: 01343 576001
M.C.Admissions@moray.uhi.ac.uk
www.moray.uhi.ac.uk

Napier University
219 Colinton Road
Edinburgh
EH14 1DJ
Tel: 0131 444 2266
Fax: 0131 455 6333
info@napier.ac.uk
www.napier.ac.uk

New College Nottingham
Pelham Avenue
Mansfield Road
Nottingham
NG5 1AL
Tel: 0115 910 0100
Fax: 0115 969 3315
enquiries@ncn.ac.uk
www.ncn.ac.uk

University of Newcastle upon Tyne
6 Kensington Terrace
Newcastle upon Tyne
NE1 7RU
Tel: 0191 222 6000
Fax: 0191 222 6139
admissions-enquiries@ncl.ac.uk
www.ncl.ac.uk

Newcastle College
Rye Hill Campus
Scotswood Road
Newcastle upon Tyne
NE4 7SA
Tel: 0191 200 4000
Fax: 0191 200 4517
enquiries@ncl-coll.ac.uk
www.ncl-coll.ac.uk

University of Wales, Newport
Caerleon Campus
PO Box 101
Newport
Wales
NP18 3YG
Tel: 01633 432432
Fax: 01633 432850
uic@newport.ac.uk
www.newport.ac.uk

North East Wales Institute of Higher Education
Plas Coch
Mold Road
Wrexham
LL11 2AW
Tel: 01978 290666
Fax: 01978 290008
mitchell.k@newi.ac.uk
www.newi.ac.uk

University of Northampton
Park Campus
Boughton Green Road
Northampton

NN2 7AL
Tel: 01604 735500
Fax: 01604 720636
admissions@northampton.ac.uk
www.northampton.ac.uk

Northumbria University
Ellison Building
Ellison Place
Newcastle upon Tyne
NE1 8ST
Tel: 0191 232 6002
Fax: 0191 227 4017
rg.admissions@northumbria.ac.uk
www.northumbria.ac.uk

Northbrook College Sussex
Littlehampton Road
Worthing
Sussex
Tel: 01903 606060
Fax: 01903 606007
enquiries@nbcol.ac.uk
www.northbrook.ac.uk

Norwich School of Art and Design
St George Street
Norwich
NR3 1BB
Tel: 01603 610561
Fax: 01603 615728
info@nsad.ac.uk
www.nsad.ac.uk

Nottingham Trent University
Burton Street
Nottingham
NG1 4BU
Tel: 0115 941 8418
marketing@ntu.ac.uk
www.ntu.ac.uk

Orkney College
UHI Millennium Institute
East Road
Kirkwall
Orkney Islands
KW15 1LX
Tel: 01856 569000
Fax: 01856 875323
www.orkney.uhi.ac.uk

University of Oxford
University Offices
Wellington Square

Oxford
OX1 2JD
Tel: 01865 279207
Fax: 01865 230708
undergraduate.ad@admin.ox.ac.uk
www.ox.ac.uk

Oxford and Cherwell Valley College
Broughton Road
Banbury
Oxfordshire
OX16 9QA
Tel: 01295 252221
Fax: 01295 250381
enquiries@banbury.occ.ac.uk
www.occ.ac.uk

Oxford Brookes University
Gypsy Lane
Headington
Oxford
OX3 0BP
Tel: 01865 484848
Fax: 01865 483616
query@brookes.ac.uk
www.brookes.ac.uk

University of Paisley
Paisley Campus
High Street
Paisley
PA1 2BE
Tel: 0141 848 3000
Fax: 0141 887 0812
uni-direct@paisley.ac.uk
www.paisley.ac.uk

Perth College
UHI Millennium Institute
Crieff Road
Perth
PH1 2NX
Tel: 01738 877000
Fax: 01738 877001
pc.admissions@perth.uhi.ac.uk
www.perth.ac.uk

University of Plymouth
Drake Circus
Plymouth
PL4 8AA
Tel: 01752 600600
Fax: 01752 232141
admissions@plymouth.ac.uk
www.plymouth.ac.uk

Plymouth College of Art and Design
Tavistock Place
Plymouth
PL4 8AT
Tel: 01752 203434
Fax: 01752 203444
enquiries@pcad.ac.uk
www.pcad.ac.uk

University of Portsmouth
University House
Winston Churchill Avenue
Portsmouth
PO1 2UP
Tel: 023 9284 8484
Fax: 023 9284 3082
admissions@port.ac.uk
www.port.ac.uk

University of Reading
Whiteknights House
PO Box 217
Reading
RG6 6AH
Tel: 0118 987 5123
Fax: 0118 378 8924
Schools.liaison@rdg.ac.uk
www.rdg.ac.uk

Richmond, the American International University in London
Queens Road
Richmond upon Thames
TW10 6JP
Tel: 020 8332 9000
Fax: 020 8332 1596
enrol@richmond.ac.uk
www.richmond.ac.uk

Robert Gordon University
Schoolhill
Aberdeen
AB10 1FR
Tel: 01224 262000
Fax: 01224 262185
i.centre@rgu.ac.uk
www.rgu.ac.uk

Roehampton University
Enquiries Office
Whitelands College, West Hill
London
SW15 3SN
Tel: 020 8392 3232

Fax: 020 8392 3470
enquiries@roehampton.ac.uk
www.roehampton.ac.uk

SAE Institute
United House
North Road
London
N7 9DP
Tel: 020 7609 2653
Fax: 020 7609 6944
saelondon@sae.edu
www.saeuk.com

University of Salford
The Crescent
Salford
M5 4WT
Tel: 0161 295 5000
Fax: 0161 295 5999
Course-enquiries@salford.ac.uk
www.salford.ac.uk

Sheffield Hallam University
City Campus
Howard Street
Sheffield
S1 1WB
Tel: 0114 225 5555
Fax: 0114 225 4023
Undergraduate-
admissions@shu.ac.uk
www.shu.ac.uk

Shrewsbury College of Arts and Technology
London Road
Shrewsbury
Shropshire
SY2 6PR
Tel: 01743 342342
Fax: 01743 342343
prospects@s-cat.ac.uk
www.s-cat.ac.uk

Solihull College
Blossomfield Road
Solihull
West Midlands
B91 1SB
Tel: 0121 678 7001/2
Fax: 0121 678 7200
enquiries@staff.solihull.co.uk
www.solihull.ac.uk

Somerset College of Arts and Technology
Wellington Road
Taunton
Somerset
TA1 5AX
Tel: 01823 366331
Fax: 01823 366418
somerset@somerset.ac.uk
www.somerset.ac.uk

South East Essex College
Carnarvon Road
Southend
SS2 6LS
Tel: 01702 220400
Fax: 01702 432320
admissions@southend.ac.uk
www.southend.ac.uk

University of Southampton
Highfield
Southampton
SO17 1BJ
Tel: 023 8059 5000
Fax: 023 8059 3037
www.soton.ac.uk

Southampton Solent University
East Park Terrace
Southampton
SO14 0YN
Tel: 023 8031 9000
Fax: 023 8022 2259
fmas@solent.ac.uk
www.solent.ac.uk

Southport College
Mornington Road
Southport
Merseyside
PR9 0TT
Tel: 01704 500606
Fax: 01704 506240
www.southport.ac.uk

St Martin's College
Bowerham Road
Lancaster
LA1 3JD
Tel: 01524 384384
Fax: 01524 384385
admissions@ucsm.ac.uk
www.ucsm.ac.uk

Staffordshire University
College Road
Stoke-on-Trent
ST4 2DE
Tel: 01782 294000
Fax: 01782 295704
admissions@staffs.ac.uk
www.staffs.ac.uk

Staffordshire University Regional Federation
c/o Staffordshire University
College Road
Stoke-on-Trent
ST4 2DE
Tel: 01785 353517
Fax: 01782 292740
surf@staffs.ac.uk
www.surf.ac.uk

Stockport College of Further and Higher Education
Wellington Road South
Stockport
SK1 3UQ
Tel: 0161 958 3100
Fax: 0161 480 6636
stockcoll@cs.stockport.ac.uk
www.stockport.ac.uk

Suffolk College
Ipswich
Suffolk
IP4 1HY
Tel: 01473 255885
Fax: 01473 230054
info@suffolk.ac.uk
www.suffolk.ac.uk

City of Sunderland College
Bede Centre
Durham Road
Sunderland
Tyne and Wear
SR3 4AH
Tel: 0191 511 6060
Fax: 0191 564 0620
www.citysun.ac.uk

University of Sunderland
Langham Tower
Ryhope Road
Sunderland
Tyne and Wear
SR2 7EE
Tel: 0191 515 2000

Fax: 0191 515 3805
student-helpline@sunderland.ac.uk
www.sunderland.ac.uk

University of Surrey
Guildford
GU2 7XH
Tel: 01483 300800
Fax: 01483 300803
admissions@surrey.ac.uk
www.surrey.ac.uk

Swansea Institute of Higher Education
Mount Pleasant
Swansea
SA1 6ED
Tel: 01792 481000
Fax: 01792 481085
enquiry@sihe.ac.uk
www.sihe.ac.uk

Swindon College
Regent Circus
Swindon
SN1 1PT
Tel: 01793 491591
Fax: 01793 641794
www.swindon-college.ac.uk

University of Teesside
Middlesbrough
TS1 3BA
Tel: 01642 218121
Fax: 01642 384201
registry@tees.ac.uk
www.tees.ac.uk

Thames Valley University
Crescent Road
Reading
Berkshire
RG1 5RQ
Tel: 0118 967 5000
Fax: 0118 967 5301
reading.enquiries@tvu.ac.uk
www.tvu.ac.uk/reading

Trinity College Carmarthen
College Road
Carmarthen
SA31 3EP
Tel: 01267 676767
Fax: 01267 676766
registry@trinity-cm.ac.uk
www.trinity-cm.ac.uk

University of Ulster, Coleraine
Cromore Road
Coleraine
County Londonderry
BT52 1SA
Tel: 028 7034 4141
Fax: 028 7032 4908
online@ulst.ac.uk
www.ulst.ac.uk

University College London
University of London
Gower Street
London
WC1E 6BT
Tel: 020 7679 2000
Fax: 020 7679 7920
degree-info@ucl.ac.uk
www.ucl.ac.uk

West Suffolk College
Out Risbygate
Bury St Edmunds
Suffolk
IP33 3RL
Tel: 01284 701301
Fax: 01284 750561
mail@westsuffolk.ac.uk
www.westsuffolk.ac.uk

West Thames College
London Road
Isleworth
Middlesex
TW7 4HS
Tel: 020 8326 2000
Fax: 020 8569 7787
info@west-thames.ac.uk
www.west-thames.ac.uk

University of Westminster
Central Student Administration
Metford House
115 New Cavendish Street
London
W1W 6UW
Tel: 020 7911 5000
Fax: 020 7911 5858
admissions@wmin.ac.uk
www.wmin.ac.uk

Westminster Kingsway College
Vincent Square
London
SW1P 2PD
Tel: 020 7556 8001

Fax: 020 7556 8003
courseinfo@westking.ac.uk
www.westking.ac.uk

Weston College
Knightstone Road
Weston-super-Mare
North Somerset
BS23 2AL
Tel: 01934 411411
Fax: 01934 411410
enquiries@weston.ac.uk
www.weston.ac.uk

Weymouth College
Cranford Avenue
Weymouth
Dorset
DT4 7LQ
Tel: 01305 761100
Fax: 01305 208892
igs@weymouth.ac.uk
www.weymouth.ac.uk

Wigan and Leigh College
PO Box 53
Parsons Walk
Wigan
WN1 1RS
Tel: 01942 761600
Fax: 01942 761533
admissions@wigan-leigh.ac.uk
www.wigan-leigh.ac.uk

Wiltshire College Trowbridge
College Road
Trowbridge
Wiltshire
BA14 0ES
Tel: 01225 766241
Fax: 01225 756364
info@wiltscoll.ac.uk
www.wiltscoll.ac.uk

Wimbledon School of Art
Merton Hall Road
London
SW19 3QA
Tel: 020 8408 5000
Fax: 020 8408 5050
art@wimbledon.ac.uk
www.wimbledon.ac.uk

Wirral Metropolitan College
Borough Road
Birkenhead

Merseyside
CH42 9QD
Tel: 0151 551 7777
Fax: 0151 551 7401
h.e.enquiries@wmc.ac.uk
www.wmc.ac.uk

University of Wolverhampton
Wulfruna Street
Wolverhampton
WV1 1SB
Tel: 01902 321000
Fax: 01902 322686
enquiries@wlv.ac.uk
www.wlv.ac.uk

University of Worcester
Henwick Grove
Worcester
WR2 6AJ
Tel: 01905 855000
Fax: 01905 855132
admissions@worc.ac.uk
www.worc.ac.uk

Worcester College of Technology
Deansway
Worcester
WR1 2JF
Tel: 01905 725555
Fax: 01905 28906
college@wortech.ac.uk
www.wortech.ac.uk

Writtle College
Writtle
Essex
CM1 3RR
Tel: 01245 424200
Fax: 01245 420456
info@writtle.ac.uk
www.writtle.ac.uk

Yeovil College
Mudford Road
Yeovil
Somerset
BA21 4DR
Tel: 01935 423921
Fax: 01935 429962
juc@yeovil-college.ac.uk
www.yeovil-college.ac.uk

York College
Tadcaster Road
York

YO24 1UA
Tel: 01904 770200
Fax: 01904 770499
callcentre@yorkcollege.ac.uk
www.yorkcollege.ac.uk

York St John University College
Lord Mayor's Walk
York
YO31 7EX
Tel: 01904 624624
Fax: 01904 712512
admissions@yorksj.ac.uk
www.yorksj.ac.uk

Yorkshire Coast College of Further and Higher Education
Lady Edith Drive
Scarborough
North Yorkshire
YO12 5RN
Tel: 01723 372105
Fax: 01723 501918
admissions@yorkshirecoastcollege.ac.uk
www.yorkshirecoastcollege.ac.uk

Non-UCAS

Aberdeen College
Gallowgate
Aberdeen
AB25 1BN
Tel:01224 612330
Fax: 01224 612001
enquiry@abcol.ac.uk
www.abcol.ac.uk

Abingdon and Witney College
Abingdon Campus
Northcourt Road
Abingdon
Oxfordshire
OX14 1GG
Tel: 01235 555585
Fax:01235 553168
inquiry@abingdon-witney.ac.uk
www.abingdon-witney.ac.uk

Accrington and Rossendale College
Sandy Lane
Accrington
Lancashire
BB5 2AW
Tel: 01254 389933
Fax: 01254 354001

info@across.ac.uk
www.across.ac.uk

Alton College
Old Odiham Road
Alton
Hampshire
GU34 2LX
Tel: 01420 592200
Fax: 01420 592253
enquiries@altoncollege.ac.uk
www.altoncollege.ac.uk

Angus College
Keptie Road
Arbroath
DD11 3EA
Tel: 01241 432600
Fax: 01241 876169
marketing@angus.ac.uk
www.angus.ac.uk

Anniesland College
Hatfield Drive
Glasgow
G12 0YE
Tel: 01413 573969
Fax: 01413 576557
reception@anniesland.ac.uk
www.anniesland.ac.uk

Armagh College of Further Education
Lonsdale Street
Armagh
County Armagh
BT61 7HN
Tel: 02837 522205
Fax: 02837 512845
enquiries@armaghcollege.ac.uk
www.armaghcollege.ac.uk

Ayr College
Dam Park
Ayr
KA8 OEU
Tel: 01292 265184
Fax: 01292 263889
admissions@ayrcoll.ac.uk
www.ayrcoll.ac.uk

Banff and Buchan College
Henderson road
Fraserburgh
Aberdeenshire
AB43 9GA
Tel: 01346 586100
Fax: 01346 515370
info@banff-buchan.ac.uk
www.banff-buchan.ac.uk

Barnet College
Wood Street
Barnet
EN5 4AZ
Tel: 020 8440 6321
Fax: 020 8441 5236
info@barnet.ac.uk
www.barnet.ac.uk

Barrow in Furness Sixth Form College
Rating Lane
Barrow in Furness
Cumbria
LA13 9LE
Tel: 01229 828377
Fax: 01229 836874
www.barrow6fc.ac.uk

Barry College
Colcot Road
Barry
Vale of Glamorgan
CF62 8YJ
Tel: 01446 725000
Fax: 01446 732667
enquiries@barry.ac.uk
www.barry.ac.uk

City of Bath College
Avon Street
Bath
BA1 1UP
Tel: 01225 312191
Fax: 01225 444213
enquiries@citybathcoll.ac.uk
www.citybathcoll.ac.uk

Belfast Institute of Further and Higher Education
The Gerald Moag Campus
125–153 Millfield
Belfast
BT1 1HS
Tel: 028 9026 5000
Fax: 028 9026 5041
information@belfastinstitute.ac.uk
www.belfastinstitute.ac.uk

Bexley College
Tower Road
Belvedere
Kent
DA17 6JA
Tel: 01332 442331
Fax: 01332 448403
courses@bexley.ac.uk
www.bexley.ac.uk

Blake College
162 New Cavendish Street
London
W1W 6YS
Tel: 020 7636 0658
Fax: 020 7436 0049
study@blake.ac.uk
www.blake.ac.uk

Borders College
Melrose Road
Galashiels
Scottish Borders
TD1 2AF
Tel: 08700 505152
Fax: 01896 758179
enquiries@borderscollege.ac.uk
www.borderscollege.ac.uk

**Bournemouth and Poole
College of Further Education**
North Road
Poole
Dorset
BH14 0LS
Tel: 01202 205205
Fax: 01202 205241
enquiries@thecollege.co.uk
www.thecollege.co.uk

**Bracknell and Wokingham
College**
Church Road
Bracknell
RG12 1 DJ
Tel: 01344 460200
Fax: 01344 460360
study@bracknell,ac,uk
www.bracknell.ac.uk

Braintree College
1 Church Lane
Braintree
Essex
CM7 5SN
Tel: 01376 321711

Fax: 01376 340799
enquiries@braintree.ac.uk
www.braintree.ac.uk

Bridgend College
Cowbridge Road
Bridgend
CF31 3DF
Tel: 01656 302302
Fax: 01656 663912
admissions@bridgend.ac.uk
www.bridgend.ac.uk

City College Brighton and Hove
Pelham Street
Brighton
BN1 4FA
Tel: 01273 667788
Fax: 01273 667703
info@ccb.ac.uk
www.ccb.ac.uk

Bristol Old Vic Theatre School
2 Downside Road
Clifton
Bristol
BS8 2XF
Tel: 0117 973 3535
Fax: 0117 923 9371
enquiries@oldvic.ac.uk
www.oldvic.ac.uk

Brooklands College
Heath Road
Weybridge
Surrey
KT13 8TT
Tel: 01932 797700
Fax: 01932 797800
info@brooklands.ac.uk
www.brooklands.ac.uk

Burnley College
Shorey Bank
Ormerod Road
Burnley
BB11 2RX
Tel: 01282 711200
Fax: 01282 415063
student.services@burnley.ac.uk
www.burnley.ac.uk

Bury College
Market Street
Bury
Greater Manchester

BL9 0BG
Tel: 0800 092 5900
Fax: 0161 280 8228
information@burycollege.ac.uk
www.burycollege.ac.uk

Calderdale College
Francis Street
Halifax
HX1 3UZ
Tel: 01422 357357
Fax: 01422 399320
www.calderdale.ac.uk

Cambridge Regional College
King Hedges Road
Cambridge
CB4 2QT
Tel: 01223 418200
Fax: 01223 426425
enquiry@camre.ac.uk
www.camre.ac.uk

**Cambridge School of Visual &
Performing Arts**
Round Church Street
Cambridge
CB5 8AD
Tel: 01223 314431
Fax: 01223 467773
enquiries@catscollege.com
www.cambridgeartschool.com

**Cannock Chase Technical
College**
The Green
Cannock
Staffordshire
WS11 1UE
Tel: 01543 462200
Fax: 01543 574223
enquiries@cannock.ac.uk
www.cannock.ac.uk

Cardonald College
690 Mosspark Drive
Glasgow
G52 3AY
Tel: 0141 272 3333
Fax: 0141 272 3444
enquiries@cardonald.ac.uk
www.cardonald.ac.uk

Carmel College
Prescot Road
St Helens
WA10 3AG
Tel: 01744 452200
Fax: 01744 452222
www.carmel.ac.uk

Castlereagh College
Montgomery Road
Belfast
BT6 9JD
Tel: 028 9079 7144
Fax: 028 9040 1820
www.castlereagh.ac.uk

Cavendish College
35–37 Alfred Place
London
WC1E 7DP
Tel: 020 7580 6043/4074
Fax: 020 7255 1591
learn@cavendish.ac.uk
www.cavendish.ac.uk

Central College of Commerce
300 Cathedral Street
Glasgow
G1 2TA
Tel: 0141 552 3941
Fax: 0141 553 2368
information@central-glasgow.ac.uk
www.centralcollege.ac.uk

Christie's Education
153 Great Titchfield Street
London
W1W 5BD
Tel: 020 7665 4350
Fax: 020 7665 4351
education@christies.ac.uk
www.christies.com

**City and Guilds of London Art
School**
124 Kennington Park Road
London
SE11 4DJ
Tel: 020 7735 2306
Fax: 020 7582 5361
info@cityandguildsartschool
www.cityandguildsartschool.ac.uk

City Literary Institute
Stukeley Street
Covent Garden
London
WC2B 5LJ
Tel: 020 7242 9872
Fax: 020 7405 3347
infoline@citylit.ac.uk
www.citylit.ac.uk

Clackmannan College of Further Education
Branshill Road
Alloa
FK10 3BT
Tel: 01259 215121
Fax: 01259 722879
learning@clacks.ac.uk
www.clacks.ac.uk

Clydebank College
Kilbowie Road
Clydebank
G81 2AA
Tel: 0141 952 7771
Fax: 0141 951 1574
info@clydebank.ac.uk
www.clydebank.ac.uk

Coleg Gwent, Crosskeys Campus
Risca Road
Crosskeys
Caerphilly
NP1 7ZA
info@coleggwent.ac.uk
www.coleggwent.ac.uk

Coleg Meirion-Dwyfor
Ffordd Ty'n y Coed
Dolgellau
Gwynedd
LL40 2SW
Tel: 01341 422827
Fax: 01341 422393
coleg@meirion-dwyfor.ac.uk
www.meirion-dwyfor.ac.uk

Coleg Morgannwg
Ynys Terrace
Rhydyfelin
Pontypridd
CF37 5RN
Tel: 01443 662800
Fax: 01443 663028
college@pontypridd.ac.uk
www.pontypridd.ac.uk

Coleg Powys
Llanidloes Road
Newtown
Powys
SY16 4HU
Tel: 01686 622722
Fax: 01686 622246
enquiries@coleg-powys.ac.uk
www.coleg-powys.ac.uk

College of North East London
High Road
Tottenham
London
N15 4RU
Tel: 020 8802 3111
Fax: 020 8442 3091
guidance@staff.conel.ac.uk
www.conel.ac.uk

College of North West London
Willesden Centre
Dudden Hill Lane
London
NW10 2XD
Tel: 020 8208 5050
courenq@cnwl.ac.uk
www.cnwl.ac.uk

Cornwall College St Austell
Trevarthian Road
St Austell
Cornwall
PL25 4BU
Tel: 01726 67911
Fax: 01726 67911
info@st-austell.ac.uk
www.cornwall.ac.uk/stac

Craven College
High Street
Skipton
North Yorkshire
BD23 1JY
Tel: 01756 791411
Fax: 01756 794872
Enquiries@craven-college.ac.uk
www.craven-college.ac.uk

Deeside College
Kelsterton Road
Connah's Quay
Flintshire
CH5 4BR
Tel: 01244 831531
Fax: 01244 814305
enquiries@deeside.ac.uk
www.deeside.ac.uk

Derby College
Pride Parkway
Derby
DE24 8UG
Tel: 01332 757570
Fax: 01332 576301
enquiries@derby-college.ac.uk
www.derby-college.ac.uk

Dumfries and Galloway College
Heathhall
Dumfries
DG1 3QZ
Tel: 01387 261261
Fax: 01387 250006
info@dumgal.ac.uk
www.dumgal.ac.uk

Dundee College
Kingsway Campus
Old Glamis Road
Dundee
DD3 8LE
Tel: 01382 834834
Fax: 01382 858117
enquiries@dundeecoll.ac.uk
www.dundeecoll.ac.uk

Dunstable College
Kingsway
Dunstable
Bedfordshire
LU5 4HG
Tel: 01582 477776
Fax: 01582 478801
enquiries@dunstable.ac.uk
www.dunstable.ac.uk

Ealing, Hammersmith and West London College
Gliddon Road
Hammersmith and Fulham
London
W14 9BL
Tel: 0800 980 2175
Fax: 020 8741 2491
cic@wlc.ac.uk
www.wlc.ac.uk

East Berkshire College
Station Road
Langley
Berkshire
SL3 8BY
Tel: 0800 923 0423
Fax: 01793 793316

info@eastberks.ac.uk
www.eastberks.ac.uk

East Riding College
St Mary's Walk
Bridlington
YO16 5JW
enquiries@eastridingcollege.ac.uk
www.eastridingcollege.ac.uk

East Tyrone College of Further and Higher Education
Circular Road
Dungannon
County Tyrone
BT71 6BQ
Tel: 028 8772 2323
Fax: 028 8775 2018
info@etcfhe.ac.uk
www.etcfhe.ac.uk

Easton College
Easton
Norwich
Norfolk
NR9 5DX
Tel: 01603 731200
Fax: 01603 741438
info@easton-college.ac.uk
www.easton-college.ac.uk

Edinburgh's Telford College
Crewe Toll
Edinburgh
EH4 2NZ
Tel: 0131 332 2491/2424
Fax: 0131 343 1218
www.ed-coll.ac.uk

Elmwood College
Carslogie Road
Cupar
Fife
KY15 4JP
Tel: 01334 658800
Fax: 01334 658888
www.elmwood.ac.uk

Enfield College
73 Hertford Road
Enfield
Middlesex
EN3 5HA
Tel: 020 8443 3434
Fax: 020 8804 7028
courseinformation@enfield.ac.uk
www.enfield.ac.uk

**Falkirk College of Further and
Higher Education**
Grangemouth Road
Falkirk
FK2 9AD
Tel: 01324 403000
Fax: 01324 403222
info@falkirkcollege.ac.uk
www.falkirkcollege.ac.uk

**Fife College of Further and
Higher Education**
St Brycedale Avenue
Kirkcaldy
Fife
KY1 1EX
Tel: 01592 268591
Fax: 01592 640225
enquiries@fife.ac.uk
www.fife.ac.uk

Filton College
Filton Avenue
Filton
Bristol
BS34 7AT
Tel: 0117 931 2121
Fax: 0117 931 2233
info@filton.ac.uk
www.filton.ac.uk

Gateshead College
Durham Road
Gateshead
Tyne and Wear
NE9 5BN
Tel: 0191 490 0300
Fax: 0191 490 2313
start@gateshead.ac.uk
www.gateshead.ac.uk

**Glasgow College of Building
and Printing**
60 North Hanover Street
Glasgow
G1 2BP
Tel: 0141 332 9969
Fax: 0141 332 5170
www.gcbp.ac.uk

Glenrothes College
Stenton Road
Glenrothes
KY6 2BR
Tel: 01592 772233
Fax: 01592 568182

ask@glenrothes.ac.uk
www.glenrothes-college.ac.uk

Grantham College
Stonebridge Road
Grantham
Lincolnshire
NG31 9AP
Tel: 01476 400200
Fax: 01476 400291
enquiry@grantham.ac.uk
www.grantham.ac.uk

Greenwich Community College
95 Plumstead Road
Greenwich
London
SE18 7DQ
Tel: 020 8488 4800
Fax: 020 8488 4899
info@gcc.ac.uk
www.gcc.ac.uk

Harrow College
Lowlands Road
Harrow
Middlesex
HA1 3AQ
Tel: 020 0909 6000
enquiries@harrow.ac.uk
www.harrow.ac.uk

Hastings College
Archery Road
Hastings
East Sussex
TN38 0HX
Tel: 01424 442222
Fax: 01424 721763
marketing@hastings.ac.uk
www.hastings.ac.uk

Heatherley's School of Fine Art
80 Upcerne Road
Chelsea
London
SW10 0SH
Tel: 020 7351 4190
Fax: 020 7351 6945
info@heatherleys.org
www.heatherleys.org

Henley College
Deanfield Avenue
Henley-on-Thames
Oxfordshire

RG9 1UH
Tel: 01491 579988
Fax: 01491 410099
info@henleycol.ac.uk
www.henleycol.ac.uk

Hereward College
Bramston Crescent
Tile Hill Lane
Coventry
CV4 9SW
Tel: 024 7646 1231
Fax: 024 7669 4305
enquiries@hereward.ac.uk
www.hereward.ac.uk

Hugh Baird College
Balliol Road
Bootle
Merseyside
L20 7EW
Tel: 0151 353 4400
Fax: 0151 353 4469
info@hughbaird.ac.uk
www.hughbaird.ac.uk

Huntingdonshire Regional College
California Road
Huntingdon
Cambridgeshire
PE29 1BL
Tel: 01480 379100
Fax: 01480 379127
college@huntingdon.ac.uk
www.huntingdon.ac.uk

Isle College
Ramnoth Road
Wisbech
Cambridgeshire
PE13 2JE
Tel: 01945 582561
Fax: 01945 582706
courses@isle.ac.uk
www.isle.ac.uk

Isle of Man College
Homefield Road
Douglas
Isle of Man
IM2 6RB
Tel: 01624 648206
Fax: 01624 648201
enquiries@iomcollege.ac.im
www.iomcollege.ac.im

James Watt College of Further and Higher Education
Finnart Street
Greenock
Inverclyde
PA16 8HF
Tel: 01475 724433
Fax: 01475 888079
enquiries@jameswatt.ac.uk
www.jameswatt.ac.uk

Jewel and Esk Valley College
Newbattle Road
Edinburgh
EH22 3AE
Tel: 0131 660 1010
Fax: 0131 663 0271
www.jevc.ac.uk

Keighley College
Cavendish Street
Keighley
West Yorkshire
BD21 3DF
Tel: 01535 618555
Fax: 01535 618556
info@keighley.ac.uk
www.keighley.ac.uk

Kendal College
Milnthorpe Road
Kendal
Cumbria
LA9 5AY
Tel: 01539 814700
Fax: 01539 733714
enquiries@kendal.ac.uk
www.kendal.ac.uk

Kensington and Chelsea College
Hortentia Centre
Hortentia Road
London
SW10 0QS
Tel: 020 7573 3600
Fax: 020 7351 0956
enquiries@kcc.ac.uk
www.kcc.ac.uk

Kilmarnock College
Holehouse Road
Kilmarnock
KA3 7AT
Tel: 01563 523501
Fax: 01563 538182

enquiries@kilmarnock.ac.uk
www.kilmarnock.ac.uk

Kingston College
Kingston Hall Road
Kingston-upon-Thames
Surrey
KT1 2AQ
Tel: 020 8546 2151
Fax: 020 8286 2900
info@kingston-college.ac.uk
www.kingston-college.ac.uk

Knowsley Community College
Rupert Road
Roby
Merseyside
L36 9TD
Tel: 0151 477 5700
Fax: 0151 477 5703
info@knowsleycollege.ac.uk
www.knowsleycollege.ac.uk

Langside College
50 Prospecthill Road
Glasgow
G42 9LB
Tel: 0141 649 4991
Fax: 0141 632 5252
enquireuk@langside.ac.uk
www.langside.ac.uk

Lauder College
Halbeath
Dunfermline
KY11 5DY
Tel: 01383 845010
Fax: 01383 845001
customerservices@lauder.ac.uk
www.lauder.ac.uk

Leeds College of Technology
Cookridge Street
Leeds
LS2 8BL
Tel: 0113 297 6464
info@lct.ac.uk
www.lct.ac.uk

Leek College of Further Education and School of Art (Moorlands College)
Stockwell Street
Leek
Staffordshire
ST13 6DP
Tel: 01538 398866
Fax: 01538 399506
admissions@leek.ac.uk
www.leek.ac.uk

Leith School of Art
25 North Junction Street
Edinburgh
EH6 6HW
Tel: 0131 554 5761
Fax: 0131 554 5514
lsa@ednet.co.uk
www.leithschoolofart.co.uk

Limavady College of Further and Higher Education
Limavady
County Londonderry
BT49 0EX
Tel: 028 7776 2334
Fax: 028 7776 1018
www.limavady.ac.uk

Luton Sixth Form College
Bradgers Hill Road
Luton
LU2 7EW
Tel: 01582 877500
Fax: 01582 877501
info@lutonsfc.ac.uk
www.lutonsfc.ac.uk

Macclesfield College
Park Lane
Macclesfield
Cheshire
SK11 8LF
Tel: 01625 410000
Fax: 01625 410001
info@macclesfield.ac.uk
www.macclesfield.ac.uk

Milton Keynes College
Chaffron Way Campus
Woughton Campus West
Leadenhall
Milton Keynes
MK6 5LP
Tel: 01908 684444
Fax: 01908 684399
info@mkcollege.ac.uk
www.mkcollege.ac.uk

Morley College
61 Westminster Road
Southwark
London
SE1 7HT
Tel: 020 7928 8501
Fax: 020 7928 4074
enquiries@morleycollege.ac.uk
www.morleycollege.ac.uk

Motherwell College
Dalzell Drive
Motherwell
ML1 2DD
Tel: 01698 232323
Fax: 01698 232527
register@motherwell.ac.uk
www.motherwell.ac.uk

Nelson and Colne College
Scotland Road
Nelson
Lancashire
BB9 7YT
Tel: 01282 440200
Fax: 01282 440274
reception@nelson.ac.uk
www.nelson.ac.uk

Newark and Sherwood College
Friary Road
Newark
Nottinghamshire
NG24 1PB
Tel: 01636 680680
Fax: 01636 680681
enquiries@newark.ac.uk
www.newark.ac.uk

Newbury College
Monks Lane
Newbury
Berkshire
RG17 7TD
Tel: 01635 845000
Fax: 01635 845312
info@newbury-college.ac.uk
www.newbury-college.ac.uk

Newry and Kilkeel Institute of Further and Higher Education, Newry
Patrick Street
Newry
County Down
BT35 8DN
Tel: 028 3026 1071
Fax: 028 3025 9662
admissions@nkifhe.ac.uk
www.nkifhe.ac.uk

North Devon College
Old Sticklepath Hill
Barnstaple
Devon
EX31 2BQ
Tel: 01271 345291
Fax: 01271 338121
postbox@ndevon.ac.uk
www.ndevon.ac.uk

North Down and Ards Institute of Further and Higher Education
Castle Park Road
Bangor
County Down
BT20 4TF
Tel: 028 9127 6600
Fax: 028 9127 6715
www.ndai.ac.uk

North Glasgow College
110 Flemington Street
Glasgow
G21 4BX
Tel: 0141 558 9001
Fax: 0141 558 9905
admissions@north-gla.ac.uk
www.north-gla.ac.uk

North Hertfordshire College
Monkswood Way
Stevenage
Hertfordshire
SG1 1LA
Tel: 01462 424242
Fax: 01462 443054
enquiries@nhc.org.uk
www.nhc.ac.uk

North Lindsey College
Kingsway
Scunthorpe
Lincolnshire
DN17 1AJ
Tel: 01724 281111
Fax: 01724 294020
info@northlindsey.ac.uk
www.northlindsey.ac.uk

North West Institute of Further and Higher Education
Strand Road
Londonderry
County Londonderry
BT48 7BY
Tel: 028 7126 6711
Fax: 028 7126 0520
www.nwifhe.ac.uk

Oaklands College
Welwyn Garden City
Hertfordshire
AL4 0JA
Tel: 01727 850651
Fax: 01727 847987
help.line@oaklands.ac.uk
www.oaklands.ac.uk

Priestley College
Loushers Lane
Warrington
WA4 6RD
Tel: 01925 633591
Fax: 01925 413887
enquiries@priestley.ac.uk
www.priestley.ac.uk

Prince's Foundation
19–22 Charlotte Road
London
EC2A 3SG
Tel: 020 7613 8500
Fax: 020 7613 8599
rsuzuki@princes-foundation.org
www.princes-foundation.org

Queen Elizabeth Sixth Form College
Vane Terrace
Darlington
DL3 7AU
Tel: 01325 461315
Fax: 01325 361705
enquiry@qeliz.ac.uk
www.qeliz.ac.uk

Reid Kerr College
Renfrew Road
Paisley
PA3 4DR
Tel: 0141 581 2222
Fax: 0141 581 2204
sservices@reidkerr.ac.uk
www.reidkerr.ac.uk

Richmond Adult Community College
Clifden Road
Twickenham
London
TW1 4LT
Tel: 020 8891 5907
Fax: 020 8892 6354
www.racc.ac.uk

Richmond upon Thames College
Egerton Road
Twickenham
London
TW2 7SJ
Tel: 020 8607 8000
Fax: 020 8744 9738
courses@rutc.ac.uk.
www.rutc.ac.uk

Royal Academy Schools
Burlington Gardens
London
W1J 0BD
Tel: 020 7300 5920
Fax: 020 7300 5856
www.royalacademy.org.uk

Royal College of Art
Kensington Gore
London
SW7 2EU
Tel: 020 7590 4444
Fax: 020 7590 4500
admissions@rca.ac.uk
www.rca.ac.uk

Runshaw College
Langdale Road
Leyland
Preston
Lancashire
PR25 3DQ
Tel: 01772 622677
Fax: 01772 642009
www.runshaw.ac.uk

Selby College
Abbot's Road
Selby
North Yorkshire
YO8 8AT
Tel: 01757 211000
Fax: 01757 213137
info@selby.ac.uk
www.selby.ac.uk

Sotheby's Institute of Art
30 Oxford Street
London
W1D 1AU
Tel: 020 7462 3232
Fax: 020 7580 8160
info@sothebysinstitutelondon.com
www.sothebysinstitutelondon.com

South East Derbyshire College
Field Road
Ilkeston
Derbyshire
DE7 5RS
Tel: 0115 849 2000
Fax: 0115 849 2121
admissions@sedc.ac.uk
www.sedc.ac.uk

South Kent College
Shorncliffe Road
Folkestone
Kent
CT20 2TZ
admissions@southkent.ac.uk
www.southkent.ac.uk

South Thames College
Wandsworth High Street
London
SW18 2PP
Tel: 020 8918 7777
studentservices@south-thames.ac.uk
www.south-thames.ac.uk

Southgate College
Southgate High Street
London
N14 6BS
Tel: 020 8982 5050
Fax: 020 8982 5051
admiss@southgate.ac.uk
www.southgate.ac.uk

Stevenson College
Bankhead Avenue
Edinburgh
EH11 4DE
Tel: 0131 535 4600
Fax: 0131 535 4666
info@stevenson.ac.uk
www.stevenson.ac.uk

Stourbridge College
Hagley Road
Stourbridge

Dudley
DY8 1QU
Tel: 01384 344344
Fax: 01384 344345
info@stourbridge.ac.uk
www.stourbridge.ac.uk

Strode College
Church Road
Street
Somerset
BA16 0AB
Tel: 01458 844400
Fax: 01458 844411
courseinfo@strode-college.ac.uk
www.strode-college.ac.uk

Stroud College of Further Education
Stratford Road
Stroud
Gloucestershire
GL5 4AH
Tel: 01453 763424
Fax: 01453 753543
enquire@stroudcol.ac.uk
www.stroud.ac.uk

Sussex Downs College, Eastbourne Campus
Cross Levels Way
Eastbourne
BN21 2UF
Tel: 01323 637637
Fax: 01323 637472
eastbourne@sussexdowns.ac.uk
www.sussexdowns.ac.uk

Telford College of Arts and Technology
Haybridge Road
Wellington
Telford
TF1 2NP
Tel: 01952 642237
Fax: 01952 642263
studserv@tcat.ac.uk
www.tcat.ac.uk

Thanet College
Ramsgate Road
Broadstairs
Kent
CT10 1PN
Tel: 01843 605040
Fax: 01843 605013

student_admissions@thanet.ac.uk
www.thanet.ac.uk

Thurrock and Basildon College
Nethermayne
Basildon
Essex
SS16 5NN
Tel: 01268 532015
Fax: 01268 522139
info@tab.ac.uk
www.tab.ac.uk

Tower Hamlets College
Poplar High Street
Tower Hamlets
London
E14 0AF
Tel: 020 7510 7510
Fax: 020 7510 9153
www.tower.ac.uk

Tresham Institute
St Mary's Road
Kettering
Northamptonshire
NN15 7BS
Tel: 01536 410252
Fax: 01536 522500
info@tresham.ac.uk
www.tresham.ac.uk

Truro College
College Road
Truro
Cornwall
TR1 3XX
Tel: 01872 267000
Fax: 01872 267100
www.trurocollege.ac.uk

Upper Bann Institute of Further and Higher Education
Lurgan Campus
Kitchen Hill
Lurgan
County Armagh
BT66 6AZ
Tel: 028 3832 6135
Fax: 028 3833 2762
www.ubifhe.ac.uk

Walford and North Shropshire College
College Road
Oswestry

Shropshire
SY11 2SA
Tel: 01691 688000
Fax: 01691 688001
enquiries@wnsc.ac.uk
www.wnsc.ac.uk

Waltham Forest College
Forest Road
Waltham Forest
London
E17 4JB
Tel: 020 8527 2311
Fax: 020 8523 2376
info@waltham.ac.uk
www.waltham.ac.uk

Warwickshire College, Royal Leamington Spa, Rugby and Moreton Morrell
Warwick New Road
Leamington Spa
CV32 5JE
Tel: 01926 318000
Fax: 01926 318111
enquiries@warkscol.ac.uk
www.warkscol.ac.uk

West Cheshire College
Eaton Road
Handbridge
Chester
Cheshire
CH4 7ER
Tel: 01244 670676
Fax: 01244 670682
info@west-cheshire.ac.uk
www.west-cheshire.ac.uk

West Dean College
West Dean
Chichester
West Sussex
PO18 0QZ
Tel: 01243 811301
Fax: 01243 811343
diplomas@westdean.org.uk
www.westdean.org.uk

West Kent College
Brook Street
Tonbridge
Kent
TN9 2PW
Tel: 01732 358101

Fax: 01732 771415
marketing@wkc.ac.uk
www.wkc.ac.uk

West Lothian College
Almondvale Crescent
Livingston
Bathgate
West Lothian
EH54 7EP
Tel: 01506 418181
Fax: 01506 489980
enquiries@west-lothian.ac.uk
www.west-lothian.ac.uk

West Nottinghamshire College
Derby Road
Mansfield
Nottinghamshire
NG18 5BH
Tel: 01623 627191
Fax: 01623 623063
www.westnotts.ac.uk

City of Westminster College
25 Paddington green
London
W2 1NB
Tel: 020 7723 8826
Fax: 020 7258 2700
customer.services@cwc.ac.uk
www.cwc.ac.uk

Winstanley College
Winstanley Road
Billinge
Wigan
Greater Manchester
WN5 7XF
Tel: 01695 633244
Fax: 01695 633409
www.winstanley.ac.uk

City of Wolverhampton College
Paget Road
Wolverhampton
WV6 0DU
Tel: 01902 317700
Fax: 01902 423070
mail@wolverhamptoncollege.ac.uk
www.wolverhamptoncollege.ac.uk

Yale College of Wrexham
Grove Park Road
Wrexham
LL12 7AA
Tel: 01978 311794
Fax: 01978 291256
admissions@yale-wrexham.ac.uk
www.yale-wrexham.co.uk